Motor Voter: The National Voter Registration Act

Robert Timothy Reagan

Federal Judicial Center
2014

This Federal Judicial Center publication was undertaken in furtherance of the Center's statutory mission to develop and conduct research and education programs for the judicial branch. While the Center regards the content as responsible and valuable, it does not reflect policy or recommendations of the Board of the Federal Judicial Center.

Contents

Introduction 1
Constitutionality 2
Federal Elections 8
Preclearance 9
Mail Voter Registration Form 11
Voter Registration Drives 18
Section 6: Mail Registration 20
Section 7: Voter Registration Agencies 24
Section 8: Voter Registration Administration 37
Section 11: Notice 52
Section 12: Criminal Penalties 53
Standing 56
Privacy 67
Conclusion 68
Appendix: National Voter Registration Act 69

Introduction

The National Voter Registration Act (NVRA) was enacted on May 20, 1993, to promote voter registration.[1] At his signing ceremony, President Clinton explained,

> I have said many times in many places that in this country we don't have a person to waste. Surely the beginning of honoring that pledge is making sure the franchise is extended to and used by every eligible American. Today we celebrate our noble tradition by signing into law our newest civil rights law, the National Voter Registration Act of 1993, which all of us know and love as "motor voter."
>
> . . .
>
> . . . Voting is an empty promise unless people vote. Now there is no longer the excuse of the difficulty of registration. It is the right of every American to vote. It is also the responsibility of every American to vote. We have taken an important step this morning to protect that right.[2]

The NVRA's thirteen sections occupy thirteen pages of Statutes at Large. Sections 2 through 12 have been codified as sections 1973gg through 1973gg-10 in title 42 of the U.S. Code, chapter 20, subchapter I-H. The NVRA applies to the fifty states and to the District of Columbia.[3]

Sections 1 through 3 contain the statute's title, findings and purposes, and definitions, respectively. The key findings are that the right to vote is a fundamental right and all levels of government have a duty to promote the elective franchise.[4] According to its stated purposes, the Act is intended to increase voter registration[5] and ensure registration accuracy.[6] Section 13, concerning the Act's effective date, has been included as a note to section 1973gg. Sections 4 through 12 contain the Act's substantive pro-

---

1. Pub. L. No. 103-31, 107 Stat. 77 (1993).
2. Remarks on Signing the National Voter Registration Act of 1993, Daily Comp. Pres. Docs., May 20, 1993, 29 WCPD No. 914.
3. 42 U.S.C. § 1973gg-1(4) (2012); Colón-Marrero v. Conty-Pérez, 703 F.3d 134, 137 (1st Cir. 2012) ("the NVRA by its terms does not apply to Puerto Rico").
4. NVRA § 2(a), 42 U.S.C. § 1973gg(a).
5. *Id.* § 2(b)(1)–(2), 42 U.S.C. § 1973gg(b)(1)–(2).
6. *Id.* § 2(b)(3)–(4), 42 U.S.C. § 1973gg(b)(3)–(4).

visions. Because the Act derives from Congress's power to regulate federal elections,[7] the Act only applies to federal elections.[8]

The Act requires states to establish procedures for voter registration (1) upon obtaining a driver's license;[9] (2) by mail;[10] (3) at government offices, including those providing public assistance or disability services;[11] and (4) at military recruitment offices.[12]

Constitutionality

From President Clinton's signing of the NVRA in 1993 through 1997, three courts of appeals determined that the Act is constitutional.

The Sixth Circuit and Michigan

ACORN v. Miller (4:95-cv-45), LaPalm v. Engler (1:95-cv-184), and United States v. Michigan (1:95-cv-386) (Douglas W. Hillman, W.D. Mich.); ACORN v. Miller (6th Cir. 96-1229)

On November 3, 1997, the U.S. Court of Appeals for the Sixth Circuit declared the NVRA to be constitutional.[13]

Michigan enacted legislation in compliance with the NVRA on January 5, 1995, but on January 10 Michigan's governor issued an executive

---

7. "The Times, Places and Manner of holding Elections for Senators and Representatives, shall be prescribed in each State by the Legislature thereof; but the Congress may at any time by Law make or alter such Regulations, except as to the Places of chusing Senators." U.S. Const. art. I, § 4.

The Constitution also gives Congress regulatory power over the selection of presidential electors: "The Congress may determine the Time of chusing the Electors, and the Day on which they shall give their Votes; which Day shall be the same throughout the United States." *Id.* art. II, § 1; *see* ACORN v. Edgar, 56 F.3d 791, 793 (7th Cir. 1995) ("This provision has been interpreted to grant Congress power over Presidential elections coextensive with that which Article I section 4 grants it over congressional elections.").

8. The Act also applies only to states that require advance registration for voting. NVRA § 4(b), 42 U.S.C. § 1973gg-2(b); González v. Arizona, 677 F.3d 383, 394 n.12 (9th Cir. 2012) (identifying as exempt states Idaho, Minnesota, New Hampshire, North Dakota, Wisconsin, and Wyoming).

9. NVRA §§ 4(a)(1), 5, 42 U.S.C. §§ 1973gg-2(a)(1), 1973gg-3.

10. *Id.* §§ 4(a)(2), 6, 42 U.S.C. §§ 1973gg-2(a)(2), 1973gg-4.

11. *Id.* §§ 4(a)(3), 7, 42 U.S.C. §§ 1973gg-2(a)(3), 1973gg-5.

12. *Id.* § 7(c), 42 U.S.C. § 1973gg-5(c).

13. ACORN v. Miller, 129 F.3d 833 (6th Cir. 1997).

order forbidding state agencies from complying with the NVRA until the federal government provided the state with the funds necessary to do so.[14] The Association of Community Organizations for Reform Now (ACORN), the Kalamazoo Chapter of the Bertha Reynolds Society, and two individuals filed a federal complaint on March 21 in the Western District of Michigan to compel Michigan's compliance with the NVRA.[15] Another two individuals and two organizations filed a similar complaint with the court on March 27, and the court consolidated the cases.[16] Project Vote was permitted, on August 22, to intervene in ACORN's case.[17] A third consolidated case was filed by the U.S. Justice Department on June 14.[18]

On December 13, Judge Douglas W. Hillman held the NVRA constitutional and granted the plaintiffs summary judgment.[19]

The court of appeals agreed.[20] The court rejected Michigan's reliance on *New York v. United States*[21] to support its argument that the NVRA is an unconstitutional unfunded mandate.[22] In *New York*, the Supreme Court declared unconstitutional a federal law designed to regulate nuclear waste by giving states a choice between two alternatives that the Court determined the federal government could not impose on states separately: either take title to nuclear waste and assume liability for the injuries it causes or regulate the disposal of nuclear waste as directed by the federal government.[23]

> The *New York* Court addressed a challenge to a Congressional exercise of its power under the Commerce Clause—a power that enables Congress only to *make* laws affecting the states. In the case at hand, we are

---

14. *Id.* at 835; ACORN v. Miller, 912 F. Supp. 2d 976, 980 (W.D. Mich. 1995).
15. Docket Sheet, ACORN v. Miller, No. 4:95-cv-45 (W.D. Mich. Mar. 21, 1995) [hereinafter *ACORN* Docket Sheet] (D.E. 1); *ACORN*, 912 F. Supp. 2d at 978, 980.
16. Docket Sheet, LaPalm v. Eagler, No. 1:95-cv-184 (W.D. Mich. Mar. 27, 1995); *id.* (D.E. 1); *ACORN*, 912 F. Supp. 2d at 978–80.
17. *ACORN* Docket Sheet, *supra* note 15 (D.E. 18); *ACORN*, 912 F. Supp. 2d at 980.
18. Docket Sheet, United States v. Michigan, No. 1:95-cv-386 (W.D. Mich. June 14, 1995) (D.E. 1); *ACORN*, 912 F. Supp. 2d at 979–80.
19. *ACORN*, 912 F. Supp. 2d 976; *see* ACORN v. Miller, 912 F. Supp. 989 (W.D. Mich. 1996) (order to cure Michigan's dilatory compliance).
20. ACORN v. Miller, 129 F.3d 833 (6th Cir. 1997).
21. 505 U.S. 144 (1992).
22. *ACORN*, 129 F.3d at 836–37.
23. *New York*, 505 U.S. at 174–77.

addressing a challenge to a Congressional exercise of its power to regulate federal elections—a power that enables Congress both to *make and alter* laws affecting the states with regard to this issue.[24]

The court of appeals rejected Michigan's argument that all plaintiffs except for ACORN should have been dismissed for failure to adhere to the NVRA's notice requirement for civil suits.[25]

The NVRA's section 11 authorizes enforcement suits by the Attorney General without a notice requirement.[26] The notice requirement for private plaintiffs depends on closeness to the next federal election: (1) within 30 days, no notice is required;[27] (2) from 30 days to 120 days out, the aggrieved person must "provide written notice of the violation to the chief election official of the State involved" 20 days before filing suit;[28] and (3) more than 120 days before a federal election, 90 days' notice is required.[29] Project Vote did not have to provide notice, because it joined the lawsuit as an intervenor.[30] The other plaintiffs were safe from dismissal because "Michigan had already received actual notice from ACORN [of the violation], and already made clear its refusal to comply with the Act until 'federal funds [were] made available to fully fund' the program."[31]

The Ninth Circuit and California

Voting Rights Coalition v. Wilson (5:94-cv-20860) and Wilson v. United States (3:94-cv-4364, 5:95-cv-20042) (James Ware, N.D. Cal.); Voting Rights Coalition v. Wilson (9th Cir. 95-15449)

The U.S. Court of Appeals for the Ninth Circuit determined, on July 24, 1995, that the NVRA is facially constitutional.[32]

---

24. *ACORN*, 129 F.3d at 836.
25. *Id.* at 837–38.
26. NVRA § 11(a), 42 U.S.C. § 1973gg-9(a) (2012); *ACORN*, 129 F.3d at 837–38; ACORN v. Miller, 912 F. Supp. 989, 983 (W.D. Mich. 1996).
27. NVRA § 11(b)(3), 42 U.S.C. § 1973gg-9(b)(3).
28. *Id.* § 11(b)(1)–(2), 42 U.S.C. § 1973gg-9(b)(1)–(2).
29. *Id.*
30. *ACORN*, 129 F.3d at 837 ("the statute pertains to those who *initiate* suits"); *ACORN*, 912 F. Supp. 2d at 983.
31. *ACORN*, 129 F.3d at 837 (second quotation alteration in original).
32. Voting Rights Coal. v. Wilson, 60 F.3d 1411 (9th Cir. 1995).

A voting rights organization filed a federal complaint in the Northern District of California's San Jose division on December 15, 1994, seeking to compel California's compliance with the NVRA.[33] California's governor, Pete Wilson, filed an action in the court's San Francisco division on December 20 seeking a declaration that the NVRA was unconstitutional.[34] The court consolidated the actions in San Jose.[35]

On March 2, 1995, Judge James Ware issued an injunction requiring California to comply with the NVRA.[36] In response to the governor's motion for a stay on appeal, the court of appeals affirmed the injunction.[37] The court of appeals rejected the governor's argument that the statute violated California's Tenth Amendment rights.[38] On January 22, 1996, the Supreme Court denied the governor's petition for a writ of certiorari.[39]

The Seventh Circuit and Illinois

ACORN v. Edgar (1:95-cv-174), League of Women Voters of Illinois v. Edgar (1:95-cv-281), United States v. Edgar (1:95-cv-433), and LULAC v. Illinois (1:95-cv-1387) (Milton I. Shadur, N.D. Ill.); ACORN v. Edgar (7th Cir. 95-1800 to 95-1803, 95-3456, 96-2830, and 96-3186)

On June 5, 1995, the U.S. Court of Appeals for the Seventh Circuit held that the NVRA is constitutional.[40]

On January 11, 1995, ten days after the deadline for the states to comply with the NVRA, the Association of Community Organizations for Reform Now (ACORN) and five other plaintiffs filed a federal complaint in the Northern District of Illinois to enforce Illinois's compli-

---

33. Docket Sheet, Voting Rights Coal. v. Wilson, No. 5:94-cv-20860 (N.D. Cal. Dec. 15, 1994) [hereinafter *Voting Rights Coal.* Docket Sheet] (D.E. 1); Wilson v. United States, 878 F. Supp. 2d 1324, 1326 (N.D. Cal. 1995).

34. *Voting Rights Coal.*, 60 F.3d at 1412; Docket Sheet, Wilson v. United States, No. 3:94-cv-4364 and 5:95-cv-20042 (N.D. Cal. Dec. 20, 1994) [hereinafter *Wilson* Docket Sheet] (D.E. 1); *Wilson*, 878 F. Supp. 2d at 1326.

35. *Wilson* Docket Sheet, *supra* note 34 (D.E. 14, showing a new San Jose case number); *Voting Rights Coal.* Docket Sheet, *supra* note 33 (D.E. 10).

36. *Wilson*, 878 F. Supp. 2d at 1328–29; *Voting Rights Coal.*, 60 F.3d at 1412–13; *Voting Rights Coal.* Docket Sheet, *supra* note 33 (D.E. 43).

37. *Voting Rights Coal.*, 60 F.3d at 1413.

38. *Id.* at 1413, 1415–16.

39. Wilson v. Voting Rights Coal., 516 U.S. 1093 (1996).

40. ACORN v. Edgar, 56 F.3d 791 (7th Cir. 1995).

ance.[41] The court assigned the case to Judge Milton I. Shadur.[42] The League of Women Voters of Illinois[43] and the Justice Department[44] filed similar actions on January 17 and January 23 respectively.[45] On February 10, these cases were also assigned to Judge Shadur as related to the first two.[46] A similar action filed by the League of United Latin American Citizens (LULAC) on March 3, 1995, also was reassigned to Judge Shadur as related to the first three.[47]

On March 28, in response to a motion joined by the other plaintiffs, Judge Shadur granted the Justice Department a summary judgment injunction.[48] The court of appeals affirmed the injunction, but struck one paragraph going beyond an injunction against violating the NVRA and specifying some details about how Illinois was to go about complying with the law.[49]

Illinois decided that it would create an NVRA-compliant system of voter registration for federal elections and continue stricter registration procedures for voting in state and local elections.[50] On October 30, the Cook County Clerk and the Illinois Federation of Labor filed an action in state court challenging the proposed two-tier registration system.[51] On May 1, 1996, a Cook County judge declared the two-tier system in viola-

---

41. Docket Sheet, ACORN v. Edgar, No. 1:95-cv-174 (N.D. Ill. Jan. 11, 1995) [hereinafter *ACORN* Docket Sheet] (D.E. 1); Orr v. Edgar, 283 Ill. App. 3d 1088, 1092, 670 N.E.2d 1243, 1246, 219 Ill. Dec. 355, 358 (1996).

42. *ACORN* Docket Sheet, *supra* note 41.

43. Docket Sheet, League of Women Voters of Ill. v. Edgar, No. 1:95-cv-281 (N.D. Ill. Jan. 17, 1995) [hereinafter *LWV* Docket Sheet] (D.E. 1).

44. Docket Sheet, United States v. Edgar, No. 1:95-cv-433 (N.D. Ill. Jan. 23, 1995) [hereinafter *United States v. Edgar* Docket Sheet] (D.E. 1).

45. ACORN v. Edgar, 880 F. Supp. 1215, 1216–17 (N.D. Ill. 1995).

46. *United States v. Edgar* Docket Sheet, *supra* note 44 (D.E. 5); *LWV* Docket Sheet, *supra* note 43 (D.E. 5).

47. Docket Sheet, LULAC v. Illinois, No. 1:95-cv-1387 (N.D. Ill. Mar. 3, 1995) (D.E. 1); *ACORN*, 880 F. Supp. at 1216–17.

48. *ACORN*, 880 F. Supp. 1215.

49. ACORN v. Edgar, 56 F.3d 791, 796–98 (7th Cir. 1995); Orr v. Edgar, 283 Ill. App. 3d 1088, 1092, 670 N.E.2d 1243, 1246, 219 Ill. Dec. 355, 358 (1996).

50. *Orr*, 283 Ill. App. 3d at 1092, 670 N.E.2d at 1246, 219 Ill. Dec. at 358; ACORN v. Edgar, No. 1:95-cv-174, 1995 WL 359900, at *1 (N.D. Ill. June 13, 1995).

51. *See* Sue Ellen Christian, *Suit Challenges 2-Tier Voter Registration*, Chi. Trib., Oct. 31, 1995, Metro Chi., at 5; Scott Fornek, *Orr Suit Charges State Abuse of "Motor Voter,"* Chi. Sun Times, Oct. 31, 1995, at 11.

tion of Illinois's constitution and laws.[52] On August 22, Illinois's supreme court stayed the ruling.[53] Illinois's appellate court affirmed the ruling on September 26.[54] As the 1996 general election approached, Illinois decided not to challenge the appellate court's decision; all NVRA-compliant registrations would be valid to vote for all offices.[55]

Judge Shadur held monthly status hearings and retained jurisdiction over enforcement of Illinois's compliance with the NVRA until early 1997.[56]

South Carolina

Condon v. Reno (3:95-cv-192) and Grass Roots Leadership v. Beasley (3:95-cv-345) (Matthew J. Perry, Jr., D.S.C.)

U.S. District Judge Matthew J. Perry, Jr., District of South Carolina, upheld the constitutionality of the NVRA on November 20, 1995.[57]

South Carolina's attorney general filed a federal complaint challenging the NVRA's constitutionality on January 24, 1995.[58] The U.S. Attorney General filed a third-party complaint to compel enforcement of the Act on February 6.[59] Voting rights advocates filed a separate federal action on February 8 to compel enforcement[60] and moved on February 15 to consolidate the two cases.[61] Judge Perry consolidated the actions and held a bench trial on February 21.[62] On December 12, he issued a correct-

---

52. *Orr*, 283 Ill. App. 3d at 1093, 670 N.E.2d at 1247, 219 Ill. Dec. at 359.
53. *Id.* at 1094, 670 N.E.2d at 1247, 219 Ill. Dec. at 359.
54. *Id.* at 1104, 670 N.E.2d at 1254, 219 Ill. Dec. at 366.
55. *See* Christi Parsons, *Edgar Abandons Motor-Voter Fight*, Chi. Trib., Oct. 3, 1996, Metro Chi., at 1.
56. *ACORN* Docket Sheet, *supra* note 41; ACORN v. Ill. State Bd. of Elections, 75 F.3d 304, 305 (7th Cir. 1996).
57. Condon v. Reno, 913 F. Supp. 946 (D.S.C. 1995); Docket Sheet, Grass Roots Leadership v. Beasley, No. 3:95-cv-345 (D.S.C. Feb. 8, 1995) [hereinafter *Grass Roots Leadership* Docket Sheet] (D.E. 12–13); Docket Sheet, Condon v. Reno, No. 3:95-cv-192 (Jan. 24, 1995) [hereinafter *Condon* Docket Sheet] (D.E. 35–36).
58. *Condon* Docket Sheet, *supra* note 57 (D.E. 1).
59. *Id.* (D.E. 7).
60. *Grass Roots Leadership* Docket Sheet, *supra* note 57 (D.E. 1).
61. *Id.* (D.E. 4).
62. *Condon* Docket Sheet, *supra* note 57; *Grass Roots Leadership* Docket Sheet, *supra* note 57.

ed opinion.[63] In March 1996, South Carolina's attorney general decided not to pursue an appeal.[64]

Federal Elections

The NVRA applies to elections that include elections to federal office.

The NVRA Applies Only to Federal Elections
Broyles v. Texas (Lee H. Rosenthal, S.D. Tex. 4:08-cv-2320; 5th Cir. 09-20290)

In a June 11, 2010, unpublished opinion, the U.S. Court of Appeals for the Fifth Circuit affirmed a dismissal by U.S. District Court Judge Lee H. Rosenthal, Southern District of Texas, of a complaint that included an allegation that a municipal election violated the NVRA, because the NVRA does not apply to elections that do not include elections for federal office.[65]

Residents of Weston Lakes, Texas, and nonresident owners of property there filed the complaint on July 25, 2008, to challenge a May 10 election establishing Weston Lakes as a Texas city.[66] Judge Rosenthal dismissed all federal claims on March 31, 2009, and she dismissed state claims without prejudice.[67]

No Standing to Enforce the NVRA for State Elections
Dobrovolny v. Nebraska (Richard G. Kopf, D. Neb. 4:96-cv-3305)

U.S. District Judge Richard G. Kopf, District of Nebraska, determined on June 5, 2000, that proponents of ballot initiatives did not have standing to challenge petition-signature requirements based on the number of registered voters as violating the NVRA because the state did not adequately

---

63. *Condon* Docket Sheet, *supra* note 57 (D.E. 19); *Grass Roots Leadership* Docket Sheet, *supra* note 57 (D.E. 41).
64. Motion, Condon v. Reno, No. 95-3218 (4th Cir. Mar. 27, 1996), D.E. 36.
65. Broyles v. Texas, 381 F. App'x 370, 373 n.1 (5th Cir. 2010), *aff'g* 618 F. Supp. 2d 661 (S.D. Tex. 2009).
66. Complaint, Broyles v. Texas, No. 4:08-cv-2320 (S.D. Tex. July 25, 2008), D.E. 1; *Broyles*, 618 F. Supp. 2d at 666–67, 673.
67. *Broyles*, 618 F. Supp. 2d at 700, *reconsideration denied*, 643 F. Supp. 2d 894 (S.D. Tex. 2009); *see* Opinion, *Broyles*, No. 4:08-cv-2320 (S.D. Tex. July 23, 2009), D.E. 51 (awarding defendants $11,875 in attorney fees).

maintain its voter registration records; the NVRA does not apply to state elections, and the plaintiffs were not aggrieved voters anyway.[68]

In the summer of 1996, proponents of certain ballot initiatives challenged Nebraska's initiative-signature requirements in federal court, claiming that it was not proper for the signature requirement to be based on the number of registered voters in Nebraska at the time that the ballot petitions are due, because that number cannot be known in advance.[69] In addition, the plaintiffs claimed that Nebraska was not adequately maintaining the accuracy of its voter registration lists, as required by the NVRA.[70] The plaintiffs prevailed on no claim.[71]

Preclearance

Future requirements for jurisdictions to have changes in voting procedures precleared by the Justice Department or the U.S. District Court for the District of the District of Columbia is in doubt. Preclearance for covered jurisdictions was required by section 5 of the Voting Rights Act.[72] On June 25, 2013, the Supreme Court declined to hold section 5 uncon-

---

68. Dobrovolny v. Nebraska, 100 F. Supp. 2d 1012, 1014, 1016–17, 1026–32 (D. Neb. 2000).

69. Dobrovolny v. Moore, 126 F.3d 1111, 1112 (8th Cir. 1997); *Dobrovolny*, 100 F. Supp. 2d at 1014–15; Dobrovolny v. Moore, 936 F. Supp. 1536, 1537 (D. Neb. 1996); Docket Sheet, Dobrovolny v. Nebraska, No. 4:96-cv-3305 (D. Neb. Aug. 12, 1996); Docket Sheet, Dobrovolny v. Moore, No. 4:96-cv-3262 (D. Neb. July 3, 1996); *see* Martha Stoddard, *Petition Organizers Deliver Signatures, 2 Lawsuits to State*, Lincoln J. Star, July 4, 1996, at A1 ("One targets the restrictions placed on petition circulators.... The second lawsuit raises issues of free speech and due process....").

70. *Dobrovolny*, 100 F. Supp. 2d at 1016 ("There are questions whether the State of Nebraska has kept and maintained a reasonably current voter registration system, including a uniform, systematic, and reasonably periodic process for maintaining the State's voter registration list, in violation of the National Voter Registration Act....").

71. *Dobrovolny*, 126 F.3d 1111 (basing the number of signatures required on the number of registered voters does not violate the federal Constitution), *aff'g* 936 F. Supp. 1536; *Dobrovolny*, 100 F. Supp. 2d 1012.

72. Voting Rights Act of 1965, Pub. L. No. 89-110, § 5, 79 Stat. 437, 439, *as amended*, 42 U.S.C. § 1973c (2012) (requiring preclearance of changes to voting procedures in jurisdictions with a certified history of discrimination and requiring that preclearance disputes be heard by a three-judge court).

stitutional, but the Court did hold unconstitutional the criteria for which jurisdictions require section 5 preclearance.[73]

The future applicability of section 5 to NVRA matters will be in the context of the Supreme Court's 1997 decision in *Young v. Fordice* that discretionary implementation of the NVRA is subject to section 5 preclearance.[74]

Section 5 Preclearance of NVRA Compliance

Young v. Fordice (3:95-cv-197) and United States v. Mississippi (3:95-cv-198) (Tom S. Lee, E. Grady Jolly, and William H. Barbour, Jr., S.D. Miss.); Young v. Fordice (U.S. 95-2031)

Any discretion exercised by a state in implementing the NVRA is subject to preclearance pursuant to section 5 of the Voting Rights Act, to the extent that the state is subject to section 5 preclearance.[75]

In late 1994, Mississippi's secretary of state prepared a provisional plan—changes to Mississippi's voter registration procedures to bring them into compliance with the NVRA.[76] These changes received section 5 preclearance from the Justice Department.[77] Mississippi's legislature, however, did not enact the legislative changes that were anticipated by the secretary, so the precleared changes did not remain in effect.[78] In its new system, Mississippi continued to apply registration changes only to registration for federal elections; voters who wanted to vote in both federal and state elections had to register using the original procedures.[79]

Four voters filed a federal complaint in the Southern District of Mississippi on April 20, 1995, claiming that Mississippi's voter registration procedures were in violation of section 5.[80] The Justice Department filed

---

73. Shelby Cnty. v. Holder, 570 U.S. ___, 133 S. Ct. 2612 (2013).
74. Young v. Fordice, 520 U.S. 273, 290 (1997).
75. *Id.* at 290.
76. *Id.* at 277.
77. *Id.* at 279.
78. *Id.* at 278–80.
79. *Id.* at 278–79.
80. Docket Sheet, Young v. Fordice, No. 3:95-cv-197 (S.D. Miss. Apr. 20, 1995) [hereinafter *Young* Docket Sheet] (D.E. 1); *Young*, 520 U.S. at 280.

an action in the same district on the same day.[81] The district court granted Mississippi's motion to consolidate the cases, and they were heard by a three-judge court.[82]

On February 9, 1996, the district court granted judgment in favor of Mississippi.[83]

> Since the differences between the New System and the Provisional Plan were attributable to the State's attempt to correct [a] misapplication of state law, the court held, those differences were not changes subject to preclearance.
>
> [Also,] the distinction between state and federal elections was due to the NVRA's own provisions, not to the State's changes in voting practices.[84]

Both the voters and the Justice Department filed notices of appeal, but only the voters pursued their appeal; the Department participated as an amicus curiae.[85] On March 31, 1997, the Supreme Court unanimously reversed the district court's decision.[86]

Mail Voter Registration Form

The Election Assistance Commission (EAC) prescribes a "mail voter registration application form for elections for Federal office."[87] The form may require only such information "as is necessary to enable the appropriate State election official to assess the eligibility of the applicant and to administer voter registration and other parts of the election process."[88]

---

81. Docket Sheet, United States v. Mississippi, No. 3:95-cv-198 (S.D. Miss. Apr. 20, 1995) [hereinafter *United States v. Mississippi* Docket Sheet] (D.E. 1); *Young*, 520 U.S. at 280.

82. *Young*, 520 U.S. at 280; *United States v. Mississippi* Docket Sheet, *supra* note 81 (D.E. 5); *Young* Docket Sheet, *supra* note 80 (D.E. 5, 12).

83. *Young*, 520 U.S. at 280–81; *United States v. Mississippi* Docket Sheet, *supra* note 81 (D.E. 7); *Young* Docket Sheet, *supra* note 80 (D.E. 38).

84. *Young*, 520 U.S. at 281.

85. *Id.* at 280; *Young* Docket Sheet, *supra* note 80 (D.E. 39–40); *see* Young v. Fordice, 518 U.S. 1055 (1996) (noting probable jurisdiction); *see also* Linda Greenhouse, *Supreme Court Roundup*, Oct. 2, 1996, at 14.

86. *Young*, 520 U.S. 273.

87. NVRA § 9(a)(2), 42 U.S.C. § 1973gg-7(a)(2) (2012).

88. *Id.* § 9(b)(1), 42 U.S.C. § 1973gg-7(b)(1).

States must accept and use this form.[89] States may also accept and use forms that meet all of the statutory requirements for the federal form.[90] A published district court opinion in 2006 held that the state's form did not have to be identical to the federal form.[91]

There is a live controversy over whether the EAC must allow states to require proof of citizenship beyond a written statement under penalty of perjury.[92]

Requiring Proof of Citizenship for Voter Registration

González v. Arizona (2:06-cv-1268), Inter Tribal Council of Arizona v. Brewer (3:06-cv-1362), and Navajo Nation v. Brewer (3:06-cv-1575) (Roslyn O. Silver, D. Ariz.); González v. Yes on Prop 200 (06-16521), González v. Arizona (06-16702 and 08-17094), and Inter Tribal Council v. Arizona (06-16706 and 08-17115) (9th Cir.); Purcell v. González (06A375 and 06-532) and Arizona v. Inter Tribal Council of Arizona, Inc. (U.S. 12-71)

The Supreme Court held on June 17, 2013, that a requirement in the NVRA that "[e]ach state shall accept and use" for voter registration by mail a federal form requiring attestation of citizenship preempts an Arizona statute requiring additional proof of citizenship.[93] If a state is required to accept and use a mail-in voter registration form that asks for attestation of citizenship but does not require further proof, then the state cannot require further proof of citizenship when accepting the federal form to register voters for federal elections.

On May 9, 2006, four months in advance of Arizona's primary election, five citizens and five organizations filed a federal challenge in the District of Arizona to Arizona's 2004 revision of its voter registration and

---

89. *Id.* § 6(a)(1), 42 U.S.C. § 1973gg-4(a)(1); Arizona v. Inter Tribal Council of Ariz., 570 U.S. ___, 133 S. Ct. 2247 (2013).

90. NVRA § 6(a)(2), 42 U.S.C. § 1973gg-4(a)(2).

91. Diaz v. Cobb, 435 F. Supp. 2d 1206, 1215–16 (S.D. Fla. 2006).

92. Kobach v. United States Election Assistance Comm'n, ___ F. Supp. 2d ___, 2014 WL 1094957 (D. Kan. 2014) (opinion filed at D. Kan. No. 5:13-cv-4095, D.E. 157), *appeals pending*, Docket Sheets, Kobach v. United States Election Assistance Comm'n, Nos. 14-3062 and 14-3072 (10th Cir. Mar. 28 and Apr. 9, 2014); *see Inter Tribal Council of Ariz.*, 570 U.S. at ___, 133 S. Ct. at 2259.

93. *Inter Tribal Council of Ariz.*, 570 U.S. ___, 133 S. Ct. 2247; *see* NVRA § 6(a)(1), 42 U.S.C. § 1973gg-4(a)(1).

identification law resulting from the passage of Proposition 200.[94] Proposition 200's revision received preclearance from the Justice Department pursuant to section 5 of the Voting Rights Act on May 6, 2005.[95] The plaintiffs objected to the procedural specifics of proof of citizenship for registration and proof of identity and residence for voting.[96]

On June 19, Judge Roslyn O. Silver denied immediate injunctive relief, holding that Arizona's new proof of citizenship requirements did not violate the NVRA: "there is no indication in the language of the NVRA itself that states are prohibited from requiring additional information, such as proof of citizenship, when processing voter registration forms."[97]

Six organizations and a member of Arizona's house of representatives filed a similar complaint on May 24.[98] The Navajo Nation and one of its members filed a third similar complaint on June 20.[99] Judge Silver consolidated the three related cases.[100]

On September 11, Judge Silver declined to interfere with the next day's primary election and denied the plaintiffs a preliminary injunction.[101] She issued findings of fact and conclusions of law on October 12.[102] On interlocutory appeal, however, a motions panel of the court of

---

94. Complaint, González v. Arizona, No. 2:06-cv-1268 (D. Ariz. May 9, 2006), D.E. 1; Purcell v. Gonzalez, 549 U.S. 1, 3 (2006); González v. Arizona, 435 F. Supp. 2d 997, 999 (D. Ariz. 2006).

95. *Inter Tribal Council of Ariz.*, 570 U.S. at ___ n.2, 133 S. Ct. at 2252 n.2; *Purcell*, 549 U.S. at 3; *see* Pub. L. No. 89-110, § 5 (1965), 79 Stat. 437, 439, *as amended*, 42 U.S.C. § 1973c (2011) (requiring preclearance of changes to voting procedures in jurisdictions with a certified history of discrimination).

96. Complaint, *supra* note 94.

97. *González*, 435 F. Supp. 2d at 1001 (D. Ariz. 2006); *see Inter Tribal Council of Ariz.*, 570 U.S. at ___, 133 S. Ct. at 2252.

98. Complaint, Inter Tribal Council of Ariz. v. Brewer, No. 3:06-cv-1362 (D. Ariz. May 24, 2006), D.E. 1.

99. Complaint, Navajo Nation v. Brewer, No. 3:06-cv-1575 (D. Ariz. June 20, 2006), D.E. 1.

100. Consolidation Order, González v. Arizona, No. 2:06-cv-1268 (D. Ariz. Aug. 4, 2006), D.E. 142, *available at* 2006 WL 2246365; Consolidation Order, *id.* (June 1, 2006), D.E. 28; *González*, 435 F. Supp. 2d at 999 n.3.

101. Findings of Fact and Conclusions of Law, *González*, No. 2:06-cv-1268 (D. Ariz. Oct. 12, 2006), D.E. 219, *available at* 2006 WL 3627297; Order, *id.* (Sept. 11, 2006), D.E. 183.

102. Findings of Fact and Conclusions of Law, *supra* note 101.

appeals enjoined application of Proposition 200 on October 5.[103] The Supreme Court vacated the injunction on October 20.[104]

On April 17, 2012, an en banc panel of the court of appeals determined by a vote of nine to two that the proof of citizenship procedure for registration is superseded by the NVRA, but by a vote of eight to one that the identification requirement for voting is not inconsistent with federal law.[105] The Supreme Court affirmed.[106]

Section 9 of the NVRA requires the EAC to "develop a mail voter registration application form for elections for Federal office."[107] The commission's federal voter registration form includes the question, "Are you a citizen of the United States of America?"[108] The form calls for the applicant's signature attesting under penalty of perjury that the applicant is a United States citizen.[109]

Section 6 of the NVRA requires the following: "Each State shall accept and use the mail voter registration application form prescribed by the Federal Election Commission pursuant to section [9](a)(2) of this title for the registration of voters in elections for Federal office."[110] In 2002, the Help America Vote Act transferred responsibilities for the fed-

---

103. Order, Inter Tribal Council of Ariz., No. 06-16706 (9th Cir. Oct. 5, 2006), D.E. 13; Order, González v. Arizona, No. 06-16702 (9th Cir. Oct. 5, 2006), D.E. 16; Order, *id.* (Oct. 9, 2006), D.E. 25, *filed as* Order, *González*, No. 2:06-cv-1268 (D. Ariz. Oct. 16, 2006), D.E. 221 (denying reconsideration); Arizona v. Inter Tribal Council of Ariz., 570 U.S. ___, ___, 133 S. Ct. 2247, 2252 (2013).

104. Purcell v. Gonzalez, 549 U.S. 1 (2006); *see Inter Tribal Council of Ariz.*, 570 U.S. at ___, 133 S. Ct. at 2252.

105. González v. Arizona, 677 F.3d 383 (9th Cir. 2012); *Inter Tribal Council of Ariz.*, 570 U.S. at ___, 133 S. Ct. at 2253.

106. *Inter Tribal Council of Ariz.*, 570 U.S. ___, 133 S. Ct. 2247.

107. NVRA § 9(a)(2), 42 U.S.C. § 1973gg-7(a)(2) (2012); *see González*, 677 F.3d at 395.

108. National Mail Voter Registration Form, *available at* Election Assistance Commission, http://www.eac.gov/assets/1/Documents/Federal%20Voter%20Registration_1209_en9242012.pdf; *González*, 677 F.3d at 396, 414.

109. National Mail Voter Registration Form, *supra* note 108; *Inter Tribal Council of Ariz.*, 570 U.S. at ___, 133 S. Ct. at 2252; *González*, 677 F.3d at 396, 414.

110. NVRA § 6(a)(1), 42 U.S.C. § 1973gg-4(a)(1); *see Inter Tribal Council of Ariz.*, 570 U.S. at ___, 133 S. Ct. at 2251; *González*, 677 F.3d at 396–97.

eral voter registration form from the Federal Election Commission to the EAC.[111]

Proof Required to Determine Citizenship

Kobach v. United States Election Assistance Commission (Eric F. Melgren, D. Kan. 5:13-cv-4095; 10th Cir. 14-3062 and 14-3072)

On March 19, 2014, U.S. District Judge Eric F. Melgren, District of Kansas, determined that the EAC was in error when it concluded that the federal voter registration form provides adequate proof of citizenship for Arizona and Kansas voters.[112]

In *Arizona v. Inter Tribal Council of Arizona, Inc.*, the Supreme Court concluded on June 17, 2013, that Arizona could not ask for more proof of U.S. citizenship than required by the EAC's federal registration form, but Arizona could "request that the EAC alter the Federal Form to include information the State deems necessary to determine eligibility and may challenge the EAC's rejection of that request in a suit under the Administrative Procedure Act."[113] On the following two days, Kansas and Arizona submitted the invited requests to the EAC.[114]

For political reasons, the commission lacked members, and its acting executive director responded on August 13 that the requests would be deferred until the commission had a quorum.[115] The two states filed a federal complaint in the District of Kansas on August 21 seeking an order compelling the EAC to grant the states' requests.[116] On December 12,

---

111. 42 U.S.C. § 15532 (2012) ("There are transferred to the Election Assistance Commission ... all functions which the Federal Election Commission exercised under section 9(a) of the National Voter Registration Act of 1993 ...."); *Inter Tribal Council of Ariz.*, 570 U.S. at ___ n.1, 133 S. Ct. at 2251 n.1.

112. Kobach v. United States Election Assistance Comm'n, ___ F. Supp. 2d ___, ___, 2014 WL 1094957 (D. Kan. 2014) (p.27 of opinion filed at D. Kan. No. 5:13-cv-4095, D.E. 157).

113. *Inter Tribal Council of Ariz.*, 570 U.S. at ___, 133 S. Ct. at 2259.

114. *Kobach*, ___ F. Supp. 2d at ___, 2014 WL 1094957 (p.3 of opinion filed at D. Kan. No. 5:13-cv-4095, D.E. 157).

115. *Id.* at ___ (pp.3–4 of opinion filed at D. Kan. No. 5:13-cv-4095, D.E. 157).

116. Complaint, Kobach v. United States Election Assistance Comm'n, No. 5:13-cv-4095 (D. Kan. Aug. 21, 2013), D.E. 1; *Kobach*, ___ F. Supp. 2d at ___, 2014 WL 1094957 (p.4 of opinion filed at D. Kan. No. 5:13-cv-4095, D.E. 157).

Judge Melgren allowed several voters' rights organizations to intervene as defendants.[117]

On December 13, Judge Melgren ordered the EAC to act on the states' requests by January 17, 2014.[118]

The EAC's acting executive director issued a decision on January 17 that the requested instructions would require applicants to submit more information than would be necessary for election officials to determine eligibility; a written statement under penalty of perjury is enough.[119] Two months later, Judge Melgren determined that "Arizona and Kansas have established that their state laws require their election officials to assess the eligibility of voters by examining proof of their U.S. citizenship beyond a mere oath."[120]

Appeals are pending.[121]

Registration Eligibility Check Boxes

Diaz v. Hood (James Lawrence King, S.D. Fla. 1:04-cv-22572); Diaz v. Secretary of State of Florida (11th Cir. 04-15539)

U.S. District Judge James Lawrence King, Southern District of Florida, determined on June 20, 2006, that voter eligibility check boxes on a voter registration form did not violate the NVRA.[122]

One plaintiff's voter registration was rejected because she did not check a box stating that she had not been adjudicated mentally incapaci-

---

117. Opinion, *Kobach*, No. 5:13-cv-4095 (D. Kan. Dec. 12, 2013), D.E. 105, *available at* 2013 WL 6511874.

118. Order, *id.* (Dec. 13, 2013), D.E. 114; *Kobach*, ___ F. Supp. 2d at ___, 2014 WL 1094957 (p.5 of opinion filed at D. Kan. No. 5:13-cv-4095, D.E. 157).

119. Memorandum Decision Concerning State Requests to Include Additional Proof-of-Citizenship Instructions on the National Mail Voter Registration Form, No. EAC-2013-4 (Elec. Assist. Comm'n, Jan. 17, 2014), *available at* http://www.eac.gov/assets/1/Documents/20140117%20EAC%20Final%20Decision%20on%20Proof%20of%20Citizenship%20Requests%20-%20FINAL.pdf; *Kobach*, ___ F. Supp. 2d at ___, 2014 WL 1094957 (p.5 of opinion filed at D. Kan. No. 5:13-cv-4095, D.E. 157).

120. *Kobach*, ___ F. Supp. 2d at ___, 2014 WL 1094957 (p.27 of opinion filed at D. Kan. No. 5:13-cv-4095, D.E. 157).

121. Docket Sheet, Kobach v. United States Election Assistance Comm'n, No. 14-3072 (10th Cir. Apr. 9, 2014) (defendants' appeal, noting that briefing was completed on July 28, 2014); Docket Sheet, Kobach v. United States Election Assistance Comm'n, No. 14-3062 (10th Cir. Mar. 28, 2014) (intervenors' appeal, same).

122. Diaz v. Cobb, 435 F. Supp. 2d 1206, 1215–16 (S.D. Fla. 2006).

tated; another plaintiff's voter registration was rejected for the same reason and for failure to check a box stating that he had not been convicted of a felony.[123] Among the claims in the plaintiffs' second amended complaint, as developed through argument, was that the signing of an oath that the applicant is eligible negates the need for the check boxes.[124]

The NVRA states that a registration form provided with a driver's license application "may require only the minimum amount of information necessary to . . . enable State election officials to assess the eligibility of the applicant . . . ."[125] A mail registration form "may require only such . . . information . . . as is necessary to enable the appropriate State election official to assess the eligibility of the applicant . . . ."[126] Judge King ruled that the purposes of the oath and the purposes of the check boxes were not duplicative.[127]

The original complaint was filed on October 12, 2004, eight days after the close of voter registration for the 2004 general election.[128] On October 26, Judge King dismissed the case for lack of standing.[129] Two individual plaintiffs declined to cure registration defects upon notice of them, the other individual plaintiff did cure and was registered to vote, and union plaintiffs had not identified specific members who had been harmed by the defendants.[130]

On September 28, 2005, the court of appeals reversed the dismissal, but the court noted that Florida law had changed in the interim.[131] In his June 20, 2006, decision, Judge King ruled that Florida's rejection of voter registrations for failure to check boxes when the correct boxes to check are implied by other information on the application also did not violate the Voting Rights Act, but the plaintiffs could attempt to replead consti-

---

123. *Id.* at 1208.
124. *Id.* at 1216; Second Amended Complaint at 44–45, Diaz v. Cobb, No. 1:04-cv-22572 (S.D. Fla. May 17, 2006), D.E. 151.
125. NVRA § 5(c)(2)(B)(ii), 42 U.S.C. § 1973gg-3(c)(2)(B)(ii) (2012).
126. *Id.* § 9(b)(1), 42 U.S.C. § 1973gg-7(b)(1).
127. *Diaz*, 435 F. Supp. 2d at 1215–16.
128. Complaint, Diaz v. Hood, No. 1:04-cv-22572 (S.D. Fla. Oct. 12, 2004), D.E. 1; *Diaz*, 435 F. Supp. 2d at 1208; Diaz v. Hood, 342 F. Supp. 2d 1111, 1112–14 (S.D. Fla. 2004).
129. *Diaz*, 342 F. Supp. 2d at 1120; *Diaz*, 435 F. Supp. 2d at 1208.
130. *Diaz*, 342 F. Supp. 2d at 1117–20.
131. Opinion, Diaz v. Sec'y of State of Fla., No. 04-15539 (11th Cir. Sept. 28, 2005), *available at* 2005 WL 2402748; *Diaz*, 435 F. Supp. 2d at 1208–09.

tutional claims.[132] Reviewing a third amended complaint,[133] on February 27, 2007, Judge King dismissed all claims except for a constitutional challenge to Florida's denial of a grace period to amend incomplete voter registration applications.[134] After a five-day bench trial in 2008, Judge King denied the plaintiffs relief, finding the firm deadline for voter registration to be constitutionally reasonable.[135]

Voter Registration Drives

Challenges to voter registration regulations sometimes allege that the regulations are inconsistent with the NVRA's promotion of voter registration. An instructive case in the District of New Mexico illuminates the NVRA's companion goal of promoting registration integrity.[136]

Validity of New Mexico's Voter Registration Regulations

American Association of People with Disabilities v. Herrera (James O. Browning, D.N.M. 1:08-cv-702)

On September 17, 2008, U.S. District Judge James O. Browning, District of New Mexico, determined that voter registration regulations passed in 2005 were not preempted by the NVRA.[137]

Specifically,[138] registration regulation does not conflict with the NVRA's stated goals of increasing voter registration and voting,[139] because purposes of the NVRA also include "integrity of the electoral process"[140] and "accurate and current voter registration rolls."[141] A requirement that third-party voter registration agents put their identification numbers on the voter registration forms was not inconsistent with the

---

132. *Diaz*, 435 F. Supp. 2d 1206.
133. Third Amended Complaint, *Diaz*, No. 1:04-cv-22572 (S.D. Fla. July 10, 2006), D.E. 170.
134. Diaz v. Cobb, 475 F. Supp. 2d 1270, 1270 (S.D. Fla. 2007).
135. Diaz v. Cobb, 541 F. Supp. 2d 1319, 1319 (S.D. Fla. 2008).
136. Am. Ass'n of People with Disabilities v. Herrera, 580 F. Supp. 2d 1195, 1241–43 (D.N.M. 2008).
137. *Id.* at 1241–43.
138. *Id.* at 1242.
139. NVRA § 2(a), (b)(1)–(2), 42 U.S.C. § 1973gg(a), (b)(1)–(2) (2012).
140. *Id.* § 2(b)(3), 42 U.S.C. § 1973gg(b)(3).
141. *Id.* § 2(b)(4), 42 U.S.C. § 1973gg(b)(4).

NVRA's requirement that federal voter registration-by-mail forms require only information required to "assess the eligibility of the applicant and to administer voter registration and other parts of the election process."[142] Also, a New Mexico requirement that registration agents submit completed registrations within 48 hours of the forms' completion did not violate the NVRA's requirement that voter registration forms be accepted if submitted "not later than the lesser of 30 days, or the period provided by State law, before the date of the election,"[143] because the regulation imposed penalties for its violation only on the registration agents and not on the voters.[144]

Judge Browning also found that the plaintiffs had not shown the regulations to be inconsistent with the First Amendment or New Mexico law.[145]

Four voter registration organizations filed the action against New Mexico's secretary of state in New Mexico's district court for the County of Bernalillo on July 24, 2008.[146] The secretary removed the action to federal court on July 29.[147] On August 11, the plaintiffs moved for a preliminary injunction,[148] which Judge Browning denied.[149] On February 5, 2010, Judge Browning granted the secretary's motion to dismiss the NVRA claim in an amended complaint for reasons similar to his denial of a pre-

---

142. *Am. Ass'n of People with Disabilities*, 580 F. Supp. 2d at 1243; *see* NVRA § 9(b)(1), 42 U.S.C. § 1973gg-7(b)(1).

143. NVRA § 8(a)(1)(C), 42 U.S.C. § 1973gg-6(a)(1)(C).

144. *Am. Ass'n of People with Disabilities*, 580 F. Supp. 2d at 1242–43.

145. *Id.* at 1226–41, 1243–45.

146. Am. Ass'n of People with Disabilities v. Herrera, No. CV 2008 07673 (N.M. Dist. Ct. Bernalillo Cnty. July 24, 2008), *attached to* Notice of Removal, Am. Ass'n of People with Disabilities v. Herrera, No. 1:08-cv-702 (D.N.M. July 29, 2008), D.E. 1; *Am. Ass'n of People with Disabilities*, 580 F. Supp. 2d at 1209.

147. Notice of Removal, *supra* note 146; *Am. Ass'n of People with Disabilities*, 580 F. Supp. 2d at 1209.

The federal court reassigned the case from Judge C. LeRoy Hansen to Judge James A. Parker, Reassignment Order, *Am. Ass'n of People with Disabilities*, No. 1:08-cv-702 (D.N.M. July 31, 2008), D.E. 5, to Judge Martha Vazquez, Reassignment Order, *id.* (Aug. 6, 2008), D.E. 7, to Judge Browning, Reassignment Order, *id.* (Aug. 7, 2008), D.E. 11; *see* Letter, *id.* (Aug. 13, 2008), D.E. 22 (informing the parties of Judge Browning's occasional contacts with the defendant secretary of state).

148. Preliminary Injunction Motion, *Am. Ass'n of People with Disabilities*, No. 1:08-cv-702 (D.N.M. Aug. 11, 2008), D.E. 14.

149. *Am. Ass'n of People with Disabilities*, 580 F. Supp. 2d 1195.

liminary injunction.[150] Final resolution of some First Amendment and New Mexico constitutional claims, however, would require evaluation of evidence.[151] On November 12, the plaintiffs agreed to dismiss the action without prejudice following the secretary's amending her voter registration regulations.[152]

Section 6: Mail Registration

The NVRA mandates that mail voter registration forms be widely available, including for voter registration programs by private entities.[153] This has resulted in federal courts sometimes enjoining improper efforts by states to regulate federal voter registrations.

The U.S. Court of Appeals for the Eleventh Circuit determined in 2005 that Georgia was improperly proscribing the bundling of mailed voter registration applications.[154] In 2012, a federal district court in Florida invalidated a requirement that registration forms be delivered to election officials within 48 hours of completion.[155] Another court determined that it was not improper, however, for Tennessee to reject a registration application from a voter who gave only a rented mailbox as an address.[156]

States are permitted to require newly registered voters to vote in person in their first election, under ordinary circumstances.[157]

---

150. Am. Ass'n of People with Disabilities v. Herrera, 690 F. Supp. 2d 1183, 1224–26 (D.N.M. 2010) ("The NVRA's stated goals include not only a generalized purpose of increasing voter participation, but also protecting the overall integrity of the electoral process and the accuracy of voter-registration rolls."); *see* Amended Complaint, *Am. Ass'n of People with Disabilities*, No. 1:08-cv-702 (D.N.M. Aug. 14, 2009), D.E. 75.

151. *Am. Ass'n of People with Disabilities*, 690 F. Supp. 2d at 1214–24.

152. Stipulation, *Am. Ass'n of People with Disabilities*, No. 1:08-cv-702 (D.N.M. Nov. 12, 2010), D.E. 135.

153. NVRA § 6(b), 42 U.S.C. § 1973gg-4(b) (2012).

154. Charles H. Wesley Educ. Found. v. Cox, 408 F.3d 1349 (11th Cir. 2005).

155. League of Women Voters of Fla. v. Browning, 863 F. Supp. 2d 1155, 1160–63 (N.D. Fla. 2012).

156. Pepper v. Darnell, 24 F. App'x 460 (6th Cir. 2001).

157. NVRA § 6(c), 42 U.S.C. § 1973gg-4(c).

Bundling Voter Registrations

Nu Mu Lambda Chapter v. Cox (William C. O'Kelley, 1:04-cv-1780) and ACORN v. Cox (Jack T. Camp, 1:06-cv-1891) (N.D. Ga.); Charles H. Wesley Educ. Found. v. Cox (11th Cir. 04-13435)

The U.S. Court of Appeals for the Eleventh Circuit held on May 12, 2005, that the NVRA forbids a state from proscribing the bundling of mailed voter registration applications.[158]

The June 18, 2004, complaint by a fraternity alumni chapter, filed in the Northern District of Georgia, charged Georgia with wrongfully rejecting a package of voter registrations that the fraternity had mailed to Georgia's secretary of state.[159] The forms were rejected because they were mailed in bulk, and the secretary understood Georgia law to proscribe private organizations' collecting voter registration forms.[160]

Judge William C. O'Kelley heard the motion on June 29.[161] Judge O'Kelley determined on July 1 that rejecting voter registrations mailed in bulk violated the NVRA.[162] The court of appeals affirmed the injunction.[163]

The court of appeals determined that section 6(b) of the NVRA recognizes private voter registration drives:[164] "The chief State election official of a State shall make [federal voter registration forms] available for distribution through governmental and private entities, with particular emphasis on making them available for organized voter registration programs."[165]

Section 6(a) requires states to accept by mail (1) "voter registration application form[s] prescribed by the Federal Election Commission" and (2) state forms satisfying federal criteria, and (3) the state must accept

---

158. *Charles H. Wesley Educ. Found.*, 408 F.3d 1349.
159. Complaint, Nu Mu Lambda Chapter v. Cox, No. 1:04-cv-1780 (N.D. Ga. June 18, 2004), D.E. 1; *Charles H. Wesley Educ. Found.*, 408 F.3d at 1351.
160. *Charles H. Wesley Educ. Found.*, 408 F.3d at 1351; Charles H. Wesley Educ. Found. v. Cox, 324 F. Supp. 2d 1358, 1361–62 (N.D. Ga. 2004).
161. Minutes, *Charles H. Wesley Educ. Found.*, No. 1:04-cv-1780 (N.D. Ga. June 29, 2004), D.E. 8; *Charles H. Wesley Educ. Found.*, 324 F. Supp. 2d at 1360.
162. *Charles H. Wesley Educ. Found.*, 324 F. Supp. 2d at 1365–68.
163. *Charles H. Wesley Educ. Found.*, 408 F.3d 1349.
164. *Id.* at 1353.
165. NVRA § 6(b), 42 U.S.C. § 1973gg-4(b) (2012).

these forms to change voters' registered addresses.¹⁶⁶ The court of appeals determined that the state's obligation to accept the mailed registration applications includes an obligation to accept them both individually and in bulk.¹⁶⁷

In 2006, a federal complaint alleged that Georgia was violating the holdings of the earlier case by requiring that voter registrations collected by private parties be individually sealed and forbidding their copying.¹⁶⁸ Judge Jack T. Camp granted the plaintiffs relief.¹⁶⁹ Judge Camp determined that the requirement of sealing and the proscription against copying meant that the plaintiffs were "unable to utilize their quality control measures to ensure that the [registration] workers are not submitting fraudulent registration applications" in violation of their First Amendment rights.¹⁷⁰

Automobile Resident Unable to Register to Vote

Pepper v. Darnell (Thomas G. Hull, E.D. Tenn. 2:00-cv-309; 6th Cir. 01-5529)

In an unpublished opinion issued on December 10, 2001, the U.S. Court of Appeals for the Sixth Circuit affirmed the dismissal of a pro se federal complaint alleging that it was improper for Tennessee to deny voter registration to an applicant who lived in his car and provided only his rented mail box as his address.¹⁷¹

The plaintiff filed his complaint in the Eastern District of Tennessee on August 25, 2000.¹⁷² The plaintiff refused to provide election officials with a specific physical location or address where he lived.¹⁷³ Federal regulations governing implementation of the NVRA require registration applicants who live in nontraditional residences to specify the geographic location of their residences:

---

166. *Id.* § 6(a), 42 U.S.C. § 1973gg-4(a).
167. *Charles H. Wesley Educ. Found.*, 408 F.3d at 1352–55.
168. Complaint, ACORN v. Cox, No. 1:06-cv-1891 (N.D. Ga. Aug. 14, 2006), D.E. 1.
169. Preliminary Injunction, *id.* (Sept. 28, 2006), D.E. 37.
170. *Id.* at 11–19.
  Observing that neither party had sought to move the case forward, Judge Camp vacated the preliminary injunction and dismissed the action without prejudice on November 7, 2008. Order, *id.* (Nov. 10, 2008), D.E. 110.
171. Pepper v. Darnell, 24 F. App'x 460 (6th Cir. 2001).
172. Docket Sheet, Pepper v. Darnell, No. 2:00-cv-309 (E.D. Tenn. Aug. 30, 2000).
173. *Pepper*, 24 F. App'x at 461.

(a) *Information about the applicant.* The application shall provide appropriate fields for the applicant's:

...

(2) Address where the applicant lives including: street number and street name, or rural route with a box number; apartment or unit number; city, town or village name; state; and zip code; with instructions to draw a locational map if the applicant lives in a rural district or has a non-traditional residence, and directions not to use a post office box or rural route without a box number;

...[174]

Too-Soon Deadline for Voter Registration Forms

League of Women Voters of Florida v. Browning (Robert L. Hinkle, N.D. Fla. 4:11-cv-628; 11th Cir. 12-13522)

On May 31, 2012, U.S. District Judge Robert L. Hinkle, Northern District of Florida, held unconstitutional and a violation of the NVRA Florida's requirement that voter registration forms collected by third parties be mailed or delivered to election officials within 48 hours of the forms' completion.[175]

The state has a substantial interest in seeing that voter-registration applications are promptly turned in to an appropriate voter-registration office. Applications that are not promptly turned in may be lost or forgotten or otherwise mishandled....

Even so, the state has little if any legitimate interest in setting the deadline at 48 hours. The short deadline, coupled with substantial penalties for noncompliance, make voter-registration drives a risky business. If the goal is to discourage voter-registration drives and thus also to make it harder for new voters to register, the 48-hour deadline may succeed. But if the goal is to further the state's legitimate interests without unduly burdening the rights of voters and voter-registration organizations, 48 hours is a bad choice.[176]

In addition to the constitutional violation, "when a state adopts measures that have the practical effect of preventing an organization

---

174. 11 C.F.R. § 9428.4 (2014); *id.* § 8.4 (2001).
175. League of Women Voters of Fla. v. Browning, 863 F. Supp. 2d 1155, 1160–63 (N.D. Fla. 2012).
176. *Id.* at 1160.

from conducting a drive, collecting applications, and mailing them in, the state violates the NVRA."[177]

The complaint was filed in Tallahassee on December 15, 2011, by the League of Women Voters of Florida, the Florida Public Interest Research Group Education Fund, and Rock the Vote.[178] Judge Hinkle's decision supported a preliminary injunction.[179] To position his ruling for an appeal, at the request of the parties Judge Hinkle converted his decision to a permanent injunction on August 30, 2012.[180] The appeal was voluntarily dismissed.[181]

Section 7: Voter Registration Agencies

All state offices providing public assistance or providing services for persons with disabilities must be designated voter registration agencies.[182] In 2012, a federal judge in Georgia determined that the state could not limit voter registration services to recipients of public assistance who appear in person.[183]

In 1998, the U.S. Court of Appeals for the Fourth Circuit determined that state university offices providing services to students with disabilities are among the state offices that the NVRA requires to register voters.[184]

---

177. *Id.* at 1162.

178. Complaint, League of Women Voters of Fla. v. Browning, No. 4:11-cv-628 (N.D. Fla. Dec. 15, 2011), D.E. 1; *League of Women Voters of Fla.*, 863 F. Supp. 2d at 1158; *see* Amended Complaint, *League of Women Voters of Fla.*, No. 4:11-cv-628 (N.D. Fla. Dec. 16, 2011), D.E. 5.

179. *League of Women Voters of Fla.*, 863 F. Supp. 2d at 1157–58, 1167–68.

180. Permanent Injunction, *League of Women Voters of Fla.*, No. 4:11-cv-628 (N.D. Fla. Dec. 15, 2012), D.E. 83.

181. Order, League of Women Voters of Fla. v. Secretary, No. 12-13522 (11th Cir. Aug. 24, 2012).

182. NVRA § 7(a)(1)–(2), 42 U.S.C. § 1973gg-5(a)(1)–(2) (2012); Harkless v. Brunner, 545 F.3d 445, 450 (6th Cir. 2008); Opinion, ACORN v. Scott, No. 2:08-cv-4084 (W.D. Mo. Dec. 17, 2008), D.E. 120, *available at* 2008 WL 5272059.

183. Ga. State Conference of the NAACP v. Kemp, 841 F. Supp. 2d 1320, 1328–32 (N.D. Ga. 2012).

184. Nat'l Coal. for Students with Disabilities Educ. & Legal Def. Fund v. Gilmore, 152 F.3d 283, *amended by* 190 F.3d 600 (4th Cir. 1998) (substituting Governor Gilmore for Governor Allen in the case name); *see* Nat'l Coal. for Students with Disabilities Educ. & Legal Def. Fund v. Scales, 150 F. Supp. 2d 845, 852–56 (D. Md. 2001) (holding that the requirement extended to other universities' students).

District courts in the Second Circuit[185] and the Sixth Circuit[186] reached the same conclusion. The U.S. Court of Appeals for the Second Circuit determined in 2000 that this requirement did not extend to private hospitals that provide Medicaid services.[187]

The NVRA also requires states to designate as voter registration agencies other offices selected from those described in the statute.[188]

Services required of voter registration agencies include distribution of mail voter registration forms, assistance in completing the forms, and transmittal of completed forms to election officials.[189]

The statute specifies that a voter registration agency may withhold assistance in completing voter registration forms if the applicant refuses such assistance,[190] but it was held by the U.S. Court of Appeals for the Tenth Circuit to be improper to withhold assistance from an applicant who leaves blank a written question offering assistance.[191]

No Response Is Not a Written Response

Valdez v. Herrera (Judith C. Herrera, D.N.M. 1:09-cv-668); Valdez v. Squier (11-2063) and Valdez v. Duran (10th Cir. 11-2063 and 11-2084)

On February 21, 2012, the U.S. Court of Appeals for the Tenth Circuit affirmed a district court determination that New Mexico violated an NVRA requirement—that providers of public assistance provide clients with voter registration forms unless the clients decline the form in writing—by failing to provide voter registration forms to clients who fail to answer a written question about whether they want a form that is embedded in the assistance application.[192]

---

185. United States v. New York, 700 F. Supp. 2d 186 (N.D.N.Y. 2010).
186. Nat'l Coal. for Students with Disabilities v. Taft, No. 2:00-cv-1300, 2002 WL 31409443 (S.D. Ohio Aug. 2, 2002).
187. Disabled in Action of Metro. N.Y. v. Hammons, 202 F.3d 110, 118 & n.5 (2d Cir. 2000).
188. NVRA § 7(a)(3), 42 U.S.C. § 1973gg-5(a)(3) (2012).
189. *Id.* § 7(a)(4)(A), 42 U.S.C. § 1973gg-5(a)(4)(A).
190. *Id.* § 7(a)(4)(A)(ii), 42 U.S.C. § 1973gg-5(a)(4)(A)(ii).
191. Valdez v. Squier, 676 F.3d 935, 943–48, 950 (10th Cir. 2012).
192. *Id.*

The July 9, 2009, complaint alleged violations by New Mexico of sections 5 and 7 of the NVRA.[193] The alleged section 5 violation was failure by New Mexico to provide voter registration forms with driver's license applications, and the alleged section 7 violation was regarding no response as a written declination by seekers of public assistance.[194] The parties announced settlement of the section 5 claim on July 1, 2010.[195] Judge Judith C. Herrera granted the plaintiffs summary judgment on the section 7 claim on December 21.[196] In addition to affirming the summary judgment, the court of appeals affirmed an award of attorney fees.[197]

State's Responsibility for Local Benefits Offices' Compliance with the NVRA

Harkless v. Blackwell (Patricia A. Gaughan, N.D. Ohio 1:06-cv-2284); Harkless v. Brunner (6th Cir. 07-3829 and 07-4164)

The U.S. Court of Appeals for the Sixth Circuit determined, on October 28, 2008, that Ohio's secretary of state and the director of Ohio's job and family services were proper defendants in an action to enforce a requirement by the NVRA that state agencies providing public benefits also provide voter registration services.[198]

Section 7 of the NVRA requires each state to "designate as voter registration agencies all offices in the State that provide public assistance."[199] On September 21, 2006, two potential voters who receive public assistance and the Association of Community Organizations for Reform Now (ACORN) filed a federal complaint in the Northern District of Ohio alleging that county offices of Ohio's Department of Job and Family Services were not providing voter registration services to persons receiving

---

193. Complaint, Valdez v. Herrera, No. 1:09-cv-668 (D.N.M. July 9, 2009), D.E. 1; *Valdez*, 676 F.3d at 938–40.

194. Amended Complaint, *Valdez*, No. 1:09-cv-668 (D.N.M. Aug. 27, 2010), D.E. 106; Complaint, *supra* note 193; *Valdez*, 676 F.3d at 938–40.

195. Settlement, *Valdez*, No. 1:09-cv-668 (D.N.M. July 1, 2010), D.E. 84; *Valdez*, 676 F.3d at 940–41.

196. Opinion, *Valdez*, No. 1:09-cv-668 (D.N.M. Dec. 21, 2010), D.E. 131, *aff'd*, 676 F.3d 935.

197. *Valdez*, 676 F.3d at 948–50.

198. Harkless v. Brunner, 545 F.3d 445, 451–58 (6th Cir. 2008).

199. NVRA § 7(a)(2)(A), 42 U.S.C. § 1973gg-5(a)(2)(A) (2012); *Harkless*, 545 F.3d at 450; Harkless v. Blackwell, 467 F. Supp. 2d 754, 756 (N.D. Ohio 2006).

financial support benefits from the offices.²⁰⁰ Named as defendants were Ohio's secretary of state and Ohio's director of the department.²⁰¹

Judge Patricia A. Gaughan granted the defendants' motion to dismiss the complaint on December 28.²⁰² Among the reasons for the dismissal was her conclusion that neither the NVRA nor Ohio law empowered either defendant to enforce section 7's requirements for the local benefits offices.²⁰³

"A person who is aggrieved by a violation of [the NVRA] may provide written notice of the violation to the chief election official of the State involved."²⁰⁴ Ohio's chief election official is its secretary of state.²⁰⁵ "Requiring would-be plaintiffs to send notice to their chief election official about ongoing NVRA violations would hardly make sense if that official did not have the authority to remedy NVRA violations."²⁰⁶ In addition, the court of appeals determined that the NVRA's requirement that the state's chief election official "be responsible for coordination of State responsibilities under [the NVRA]"²⁰⁷ entrusts Ohio's secretary of state with responsibility for NVRA compliance by local state offices.²⁰⁸

The NVRA and Ohio law also require the job and family services director to ensure NVRA compliance by the director's local offices.²⁰⁹

> (B) Regardless of whether a family services duty is performed by a county family services agency . . . the department of job and family services may take action under division (C) of this section against the responsible county grantee if the department determines any of the following are the case:
>
> . . .
>
> (3) A requirement for the family services duty established by the department or any of the following is not complied with: *a federal or state law* . . . .²¹⁰

---

200. Complaint, Harkless v. Blackwell, No. 2:06-cv-2284 (N.D. Ohio Sept. 21, 2006), D.E. 1.
201. *Id.*; *Harkless*, 467 F. Supp. 2d at 756.
202. *Harkless*, 467 F. Supp. 2d 754; *Harkless*, 545 F.3d at 448.
203. *Harkless*, 467 F. Supp. 2d at 762–69.
204. NVRA § 11(b)(1), 42 U.S.C. § 1973gg-9(b)(1); *see Harkless*, 545 F.3d at 452.
205. Ohio Rev. Code § 3501.04; *Harkless*, 545 F.3d at 450.
206. *Harkless*, 545 F.3d at 453.
207. NVRA § 10, 42 U.S.C. § 1973gg-8.
208. *Harkless*, 545 F.3d at 451–52.
209. *Id.* at 455–58.

The court of appeals remanded the case to the district court to provide the plaintiffs with an opportunity to amend their complaint to cure what the district court found to be defects in ACORN's standing.[211] Following ACORN's bankruptcy in 2010,[212] the case settled in 2011.[213] On May 31, Judge Gaughan awarded the plaintiffs $664,646.10 in attorney fees and costs.[214]

Medicaid Service Providers

ACORN v. Pataki (1:96-cv-1260), Disabled in Action of Metropolitan New York (1:96-cv-7661), and United States v. New York (1:96-cv-5562) (Frederic Block, E.D.N.Y.); Disabled in Action of Metropolitan New York (2d Cir. 98-9536)

The U.S. Court of Appeals for the Second Circuit determined on January 26, 2000, that state and local Medicaid offices had to provide voter registration services, but private hospitals providing Medicaid services did not.[215]

The Association of Community Organizations for Reform Now (ACORN) filed a federal action in the Eastern District of New York on March 20, 1996, seeking to expand the provision of voter registration services in New York.[216] Similar actions were filed in the Southern District of New York by advocates for the disabled on October 9[217] and in the Eastern District of New York by the Justice Department on November 13.[218]

---

210. *Id.* at 455 (quoting Ohio Rev. Code § 5101.24, emphasis by the court).

211. *Id.* at 458–59.

212. *See* Order to Show Cause, Harkless v. Husted, No. 2:06-cv-2284 (N.D. Ohio Dec. 17, 2010), D.E. 132; *see also* Michael A. Memoli, *Voter Organizer ACORN Filing for Bankruptcy*, Pittsburgh Post-Gazette, Nov. 3, 2010, at A12.

213. Judgment, *Harkless*, No. 2:06-cv-2284 (N.D. Ohio Mar. 22, 2011), D.E. 138.

214. Order, *id.* (May 31, 2011), D.E. 146, *available at* 2011 WL 2149138.

215. Disabled in Action of Metro. N.Y. v. Hammons, 202 F.3d 110, 118 & n.5 (2d Cir. 2000).

216. Docket Sheet, ACORN v. Pataki, No. 1:96-cv-1260 (E.D.N.Y. Mar. 20, 1996) (D.E. 1); *Disabled in Action*, 202 F.3d at 118 & n.5.

217. Docket Sheet, Disabled in Action of Metro. N.Y. v. Hammons, No. 1:96-cv-7661 (S.D.N.Y. Oct. 9, 1996) (D.E. 1); *Disabled in Action*, 202 F.3d at 114, 118; *see* United States v. New York, 3 F. Supp. 2d 298, 299–300, 305 (E.D.N.Y. 1998).

218. Docket Sheet, United States v. New York, No. 1:96-cv-5562 (E.D.N.Y. Nov. 13, 1996) (D.E. 1); *Disabled in Action*, 202 F.3d at 114, 118; *United States v. New York*, 3 F. Supp. 2d at 300, 306.

On November 25, the Southern District case was transferred to the Eastern District on the parties' request.[219]

On May 7, 1998, Judge Frederic Block determined that the State of New York was not required to designate as voter registration sites all facilities, both public and private, that process Medicaid applications.[220] The court of appeals affirmed, with the exception of "a small number of public hospitals operated by the New York City Health and Hospitals Corporation. As offices of local government in New York State that provide public assistance, these hospitals must be designated as mandatory [voter registration agencies]."[221]

Section 7 of the NVRA requires each state to "designate as voter registration agencies all offices in the State that provide public assistance."[222] In addition, each state must designate "other offices with the State as voter registration agencies," and the other designated offices may include types of offices listed in subsection 7(a)(3)(B).[223]

Application of this provision to private entities is not mandatory: "all nongovernmental entities are encouraged" to "cooperate with the States in carrying out" the NVRA's mandates "to the greatest extent practicable."[224] Military recruitment offices must be designated as voter registration agencies,[225] and other federal offices "shall, to the greatest extent practicable, cooperate with the States in carrying out" the NVRA's mandates.[226]

The plaintiffs urged the courts to require New York to designate as voter registration agencies approximately 1,600 public and private hospi-

---

219. Disabled in Action of Metro. N.Y. v. Hammons, No. 1:96-cv-7661, 1996 WL 684214 (S.D.N.Y. Nov. 25, 1996); *Disabled in Action*, 202 F.3d at 118; *United States v. New York*, 3 F. Supp. 2d at 305.

220. *United States v. New York*, 3 F. Supp. 2d 298.

221. *Disabled in Action*, 202 F.3d at 120; *see* United States v. New York, 255 F. Supp. 2d 73, 75 (E.D.N.Y. 2003).

222. NVRA § 7(a)(2)(A), 42 U.S.C. § 1973gg-5(a)(2)(A) (2012).

223. *Id.* § 7(a)(3), 42 U.S.C. § 1973-gg-5(a)(3).

224. *Id.* § 7(b), 42 U.S.C. § 1973-gg-5(b); *Disabled in Action*, 202 F.3d at 115, 119; *United States v. New York*, 3 F. Supp. 2d at 301 ("Thus, the NVRA clearly provides that non-governmental offices must consent before they can be designated as discretionary voter registration sites.").

225. NVRA § 7(c)(2), 42 U.S.C. § 1973gg-5(c)(2); *Disabled in Action*, 202 F.3d at 119 n.6.

226. NVRA § 7(b), 42 U.S.C. § 1973gg-5(b).

tals, nursing homes, clinics, community-based organizations, and other offices in New York City that help people apply for Medicaid.[227]

The court of appeals instructed the district court to determine which among a few dozen offices providing Medicaid services had to be designated voter registration agencies:

(1) "Any PCAP [prenatal care assistance program] provider that is an office of State or local government must be designated as a VRA [voter registration agency]."[228] "[T]hese offices provide Medicaid application forms, assist applicants in completing the forms and collecting required documentation, and transmit completed applications to [the New York State Department of Social Services]."[229]

(2) New York's Medicaid program is known as MAP—its Medical Assistance Program.[230] "Any PCAP provider that is a federal or nongovernmental office, but houses a MAP office on its premises, need not be designated a mandatory VRA. However, if the MAP office in any such PCAP provider assists or interviews Medicaid applicants, the MAP office—but not the PCAP provider—must be designated as a mandatory VRA."[231]

Many of the plaintiffs' claims in these cases were resolved by settlement.[232] On March 26, 2003, Judge Block closed out the litigation by resolving one remaining issue.[233] Judge Block rejected defense arguments by New York's Office of Temporary and Disability assistance and the New York State Office for the Aging that the state agencies are not responsible for ensuring compliance with the NVRA by their district offices, which are run by local municipal governments.[234]

---

227. *Disabled in Action*, 202 F.3d at 114; *United States v. New York*, 3 F. Supp. 2d at 299.
228. *Disabled in Action*, 202 F.3d at 121.
229. *Id.* at 116.
230. *Id.* at 115.
231. *Id.* at 121.
232. United States v. New York, 255 F. Supp. 2d 73, 74 (E.D.N.Y. 2003).
233. *Id.* at 81.
234. *Id.* at 79–81.

State University Disability Services Offices

National Coalition for Students with Disabilities Education and Legal Defense Fund v. Allen (Claude M. Hilton, E.D. Va. 1:96-cv-1379; 4th Cir. 97-1480)

The U.S. Court of Appeals for the Fourth Circuit, on July 24, 1998, determined that state university offices providing services to students with disabilities are among the state offices that the NVRA requires to register voters.[235]

An apparently prospective disabled student visiting George Mason University, a state school in Fairfax, Virginia, discovered that its Office of Disability Support Services did not provide voter registration services.[236] The NVRA requires each state to "designate as voter registration agencies . . . all offices in the State that provide State-funded programs primarily engaged in providing services to persons with disabilities."[237] The Act provides a private right of action to enforce it if the violation is not corrected within 90 days of written notice of the violation—20 days if a federal election is less than 120 days away.[238] The prospective student gave George Mason notice of its violation on July 17, 1996; because the university took no action to cure its violation, the National Coalition for Students with Disabilities Education and Legal Defense Fund (NCSD) filed a federal complaint in the Eastern District of Virginia against the governor of Virginia and other state officials on September 26.[239]

On March 10, 1997, Judge Claude M. Hilton granted summary judgment to Virginia, reasoning that state universities are not primarily engaged in providing services to persons with disabilities.[240] The court of appeals determined that state university disability services offices are covered by the Act if they are state funded.[241] The court remanded the case

---

235. Nat'l Coal. for Students with Disabilities Educ. & Legal Def. Fund v. Gilmore, 152 F.3d 283, *amended by* 190 F.3d 600 (4th Cir. 1998) (substituting Governor Gilmore for Governor Allen in the case name); *see* NVRA § 7(a)(1)(B), 42 U.S.C. § 1973-5(a)(1)(B) (2012).

236. *NCSD*, 152 F.3d at 286; Nat'l Coal. for Students with Disabilities Educ. & Legal Def. Fund v. Allen, 961 F. Supp. 129, 130 (E.D. Va. 1997).

237. NVRA § 7(a)(1)(B); 42 U.S.C. § 1973-5(a)(1)(B).

238. *Id.* § 11(b)(2), 42 U.S.C. § 1973gg-9(b)(2).

239. Docket Sheet, Nat'l Coal. for Students with Disabilities Educ. & Legal Def. Fund v. Allen, No. 1:96-cv-1379 (E.D. Va. Sept. 26, 1996) (D.E. 1); *NCSD*, 152 F.3d at 286.

240. *NCSD*, 961 F. Supp. at 131.

241. *NCSD*, 152 F.3d 283.

for a determination of which disability services offices in Virginia's state universities were state funded.[242]

On March 13, 2000, Judge Hilton issued a consent order listing which state college and university offices in Virginia would provide voter registration services.[243] Judge Hilton awarded NCSD $81,500 in attorney fees and expenses.[244]

Requiring Voter Registration Assistance for Remote Public Assistance Recipients

Georgia State Conference of the NAACP v. Kemp (Charles A. Pannell, Jr., N.D. Ga. 1:11-cv-1849)

On January 30, 2012, U.S. District Judge Charles A. Pannell, Jr., Northern District of Georgia, determined that Georgia's statutory provision for providing voter registration materials to persons receiving public assistance services only if they appear in person was inadequate, because the NVRA requires the provision of voter registration materials whether prospective voters appear in person or remotely.[245]

Two organizations advocating voters' rights filed a federal complaint in the Northern District of Georgia on June 6, 2011, accusing Georgia of "failing to ensure that all clients who apply, recertify, renew, or change an address in connection with public assistance benefits be provided with a voter preference form, a voter application form, and assistance in completing a voter application form."[246] On October 5, 2011, the federal government filed a brief in opposition to Georgia's motion to dismiss the complaint.[247]

In denying in part Georgia's motion to dismiss the complaint, Judge Pannell determined,

---

242. *Id.* at 293–94.
243. Docket Sheet, *supra* note 239 (D.E. 69).
244. *Id.*
245. Ga. State Conference of the NAACP v. Kemp, 841 F. Supp. 2d 1320, 1328–32 (N.D. Ga. 2012).
246. Complaint, Ga. State Conference of the NAACP v. Kemp, No. 1:11-cv-1849 (N.D. Ga. June 6, 2011), D.E. 1; *see* Amended Complaint, *id.* (July 13, 2011), D.E. 20 (adding a voter as a plaintiff).
247. Government Brief, *id.* (Oct. 5, 2011), D.E. 39.

There is no clear textual basis in the operative language of Section 7 paragraph (a)(6) for the proviso found in the Georgia statute implementing the NVRA, which limits the application of the mandatory distribution of forms to only those instances "when such application, recertification, renewal, or change of address is made **in person**."[248]

The parties filed a settlement agreement on April 18, 2012,[249] which Judge Pannell approved on April 26.[250]

Voluntary Cessation Did Not Moot Liability

National Coalition for Students with Disabilities Education and Legal Defense Fund v. Pataki (1:00-cv-1686) and United States v. New York (5:04-cv-428) (Norman A. Mordue, N.D.N.Y.)

U.S. District Judge Norman A. Mordue, Northern District of New York, held on March 22, 2010, that New York's voluntarily designating state college disabled student services offices as voter registration agencies did not moot an action by the federal government to enforce an NVRA requirement that the offices be so designated.[251] Judge Mordue rejected New York's argument that college offices for disabled students were exempt from the NVRA requirement because they were primarily education offices.[252]

The Justice Department filed the complaint on April 15, 2004, alleging, "The State of New York has failed to designate the [disability services offices] at SUNY and CUNY institutions, including community colleges, as mandatory voter registration agencies under Section 7 of the NVRA."[253] On March 27, 2007, Judge Mordue dismissed some of the defendants, including the governor.[254] On that day, Judge Mordue also dismissed a November 6, 2000, complaint filed by the National Coalition for

---

248. *Ga. State Conference of the NAACP*, 841 F. Supp. 2d at 1329 (quoting, with added emphasis, O.C.G.A. § 21-2-222(f)).

249. Settlement Agreement, *Ga. State Conference of the NAACP*, No. 1:11-cv-1849 (N.D. Ga. Apr. 18, 2012), D.E. 55.

250. Order, *id.* (Apr. 26, 2012), D.E. 56.

251. United States v. New York, 700 F. Supp. 2d 186, 197–99 (N.D.N.Y. 2010).

252. *Id.* at 203.

253. Complaint at 5, United States v. New York, No. 5:04-cv-428 (N.D.N.Y. Apr. 15, 2004), D.E. 1; *United States v. New York*, 700 F. Supp. 2d at 196.

254. Opinion, *United States v. New York*, No. 5:04-cv-428 (N.D.N.Y. Mar. 27, 2007), D.E. 44, *available at* 2007 WL 951576.

Students with Disabilities Education and Legal Defense Fund for lack of standing.[255]

> Defendant contends that plaintiff cannot prove that it is a *bona fide* organization rather than merely an alter-ego for [its former counsel]. ... The evidence on which defendant relies to support its contention that plaintiff cannot prove that it is a *bona fide* organization includes glaring and unexplained discrepancies in key corporate documents, lack of corporate records, pervasive disregard of corporate formalities, and suspect claims concerning plaintiff's corporate organization and membership status. ...
>
> ...
>
> In the first instance, the Court notes that the record contains scant evidence, if any, demonstrating that NCSD has any *bona fide* members.[256]

On July 8, 2010, the federal and state governments entered into a consent decree on remedies,[257] and on September 7 New York appealed Judge Mordue's liability decision.[258] The parties settled the appeal.[259]

The State's Secretary of State Was Not a Necessary Party
ACORN v. Scott (Nanette K. Laughrey, W.D. Mo. 2:08-cv-4084)

U.S. District Judge Nanette K. Laughrey, Western District of Missouri, ruled on December 17, 2008, that Missouri's secretary of state was not a necessary party in a suit to enforce the state's department of social services's obligation to provide voter registration services to its clients.[260] "The Secretary's absence from this litigation does not affect this court's ability to accord complete relief among existing parties."[261]

---

255. Opinion, Nat'l Coal. for Students with Disabilities Educ. & Legal Def. Fund v. Pataki, No. 1:00-cv-1686 (N.D.N.Y. Oct. 28, 2002), D.E. 135, *available at* 2007 WL 951559.

256. *Id.* at 10, 15.

257. Consent Decree, *United States v. New York*, No. 5:04-cv-428 (N.D.N.Y. July 8, 2010), D.E. 112.

258. Notice of Appeal, *id.* (Sept. 7, 2010), D.E. 113.

259. Order, New York v. United States, No. 10-3602 (2d Cir. Nov. 20, 2013), D.E. 148.

260. Opinion, ACORN v. Scott, No. 2:08-cv-4084 (W.D. Mo. Dec. 17, 2008), D.E. 120, *available at* 2008 WL 5272059.

261. *Id.* at 4–5.

A person eligible to register to vote and eligible for public benefits and a public interest organization filed the federal complaint in the Western District of Missouri on April 23.[262] Named as defendants were two executives of the state's department of social services and boards of election commissioners, along with their members, for three localities: Kansas City, on the state's western border, Jackson County, the county that includes Kansas City, and St. Louis, on the state's eastern border.[263]

On July 15, Judge Laughrey granted the plaintiffs a preliminary injunction against the state officers, setting a schedule for verifiable compliance with the NVRA's section 7 requirements that "all offices in the State that provide public assistance" provide its clients with voter registration assistance.[264] Judge Laughrey found that the organizational plaintiff had standing to seek relief on behalf of its members.[265] The plaintiffs, however, did not establish that the local election authorities were failing to comply with the NVRA, so the preliminary injunction did not apply to them.[266]

On September 30, the St. Louis defendants filed their unsuccessful motion to join the secretary of state,[267] a motion that the state defendants opposed.[268] The case settled on June 25, 2009.[269]

State College and University Disability Services Offices in Ohio

National Coalition for Students with Disabilities Education and Legal Defense Fund v. Taft (Edmund A. Sargus, S.D. Ohio 2:00-cv-1300)

On August 1, 2002, U.S. District Judge Edmund A. Sargus, Southern District of Ohio, determined that the NVRA required Ohio's secretary of

---

262. Complaint, *ACORN*, No. 2:08-cv-4084 (W.D. Mo. Apr. 23, 2008), D.E. 1.
263. *Id.*
264. Preliminary Injunction Opinion, *id.* (July 15, 2008), D.E. 99, *available at* 2008 WL 2787931; *see* Transcript, *id.* (July 9, 2008, filed Apr. 24, 2009), D.E. 130.
265. Preliminary Injunction Opinion, *supra* note 264, at 15–16.
266. *Id.* at 1 & n.1.
267. Joinder Motion, *ACORN*, No. 2:08-cv-4084 (W.D. Mo. Sept. 30, 2008), D.E. 108.
268. Joinder Opposition, *id.* (Oct. 15, 2008), D.E. 114.
269. Settlement Agreement, *id.* (June 25, 2009), D.E. 133.

state to designate disability services offices at the state's public universities and colleges as voter registration sites.[270]

The plaintiffs filed their federal complaint on November 6, 2000.[271] In June 2002, the secretary designated the state's college disability services offices as voter registration sites while maintaining that he was under no legal obligation to do so.[272] Judge Sargus determined that the secretary's voluntary compliance with the NVRA after the action was brought did not moot the case.[273]

Voter Registration Services for Other Universities' Students
National Coalition for Students with Disabilities Education and Legal Defense Fund v. University of Maryland at College Park (Alexander Williams, Jr., D. Md. 8:00-cv-3309)

U.S. District Judge Alexander Williams, Jr., District of Maryland, held on July 5, 2001, that the University of Maryland's obligations under the NVRA for its Office of Disability Support Services to provide voter registration services to disabled students extended to students that were not enrolled at the University of Maryland.[274]

The National Coalition for Students with Disabilities Education and Legal Defense Fund filed a federal complaint against the University and

---

270. Nat'l Coal. for Students with Disabilities v. Taft, No. 2:00-cv-1300, 2002 WL 31409443, at *7 (S.D. Ohio Aug. 2, 2002).

Judge Sargus heard and decided the matter on August 1, 2002, and issued his opinion supporting his decision on the following day. *Id.* at *1.

271. Docket Sheet, Nat'l Coal. for Students with Disabilities Educ. & Legal Def. Fund v. Taft, No. 2:00-cv-1300, (S.D. Ohio Nov. 6, 2000) (D.E. 1).

272. *Nat'l Coal. for Students with Disabilities*, 2002 WL 31409443, at *1, *4.

273. *Id.* at *6.

On September 24, 2001, Judge Sargus dismissed Ohio's governor as a defendant because of Eleventh Amendment immunity and because the NVRA does not impose obligations on the governor. Nat'l Coal. for Students with Disabilities Educ. & Legal Def. Fund v. Taft, No. 2:00-cv-1300, 2001 WL 1681115 (S.D. Ohio Sept. 24, 2001).

274. Nat'l Coal. for Students with Disabilities Educ. & Legal Def. Fund v. Scales, 150 F. Supp. 2d 845, 852–56 (D. Md. 2001).

its officials on November 6, 2000.[275] An amended complaint omitted the university as a defendant.[276]

Ruling on the defendants' motion for summary judgment, Judge Williams determined that the office was an agency that the NVRA required to be a voter registration agency.[277] Judge Williams also determined that Congress intended the office to provide voter registration services broadly, including to students not registered at the university: "Neither the statute nor the legislative history indicates a congressional intent for these agencies to implement the NVRA in a fashion that adds additional barriers to the registration of disabled persons, a distinctly targeted population."[278]

Judge Williams approved a stipulated settlement of the case on February 21, 2002.[279]

Section 8: Voter Registration Administration

The first goal of the NVRA is the promotion of voter registration: "In the administration of voter registration for elections for Federal office, each State shall ensure that any eligible applicant is registered to vote in an election . . . ."[280] A second goal is voter registration integrity.[281]

In 2013, a divided panel of the U.S. Court of Appeals for the Fifth Circuit held certain regulations of private deputy registrars were not in conflict with the NVRA.[282] Registration integrity efforts, however, must be "uniform, nondiscriminatory, and in compliance with the Voting Rights Act."[283] In 2006, a federal district judge in Ohio invalidated new

---

275. Docket Sheet, Nat'l Coal. for Students with Disabilities Educ. & Legal Def. Fund v. University of Md. at College Park, No. 8:00-cv-3309 (D. Md. Nov. 6, 2000) (D.E. 1); *Nat'l Coal. for Students with Disabilities*, 150 F. Supp. 2d at 846.

276. Docket Sheet, *supra* note 275 (D.E. 11, filed Feb. 6, 2001).

277. *Nat'l Coal. for Students with Disabilities*, 150 F. Supp. 2d at 852.

278. *Id.*

279. Order, *Nat'l Coal. for Students with Disabilities*, No. 8:00-cv-3309 (D. Md. Feb. 22, 2002), D.E. 100.

280. NVRA § 8(a)(1), 42 U.S.C. § 1973gg-6(a)(1) (2012).

281. *Id.* § 8, 42 U.S.C. § 19733gg-6.

282. Voting for Am., Inc. v. Steen, 732 F.3d 382, 399–400 (5th Cir. 2013).

283. NVRA § 8(b)(1), 42 U.S.C. § 1973gg-6(b)(1).

regulations that imposed greater requirements on paid voter registration workers than volunteer voter registration workers.[284]

District judges in Montana[285] and Michigan[286] found that the NVRA proscribed coarse reliance on changes of address for nullification of voter registrations. Registration nullifications must be designed to avoid errors. A district judge in Colorado found that Colorado's annulling new registrations for notices returned as undeliverable did not violate the NVRA.[287]

States must thin out their voter registration rolls by removing registrations no longer valid.[288] The NVRA proscribes, however, systematic purges less than ninety days before a federal election, because systematic purges close to an election do not allow for enough time to correct errors.[289]

Error correction entitled an organization advocating voter registration to inspect voter registration records to determine whether voter registration was improperly denied.[290]

Purging Voter Registrations for Noncitizens

United States v. Florida (Robert L. Hinkle, N.D. Fla. 4:12-cv-285) and Arcia v. Detzner (William J. Zloch, S.D. Fla. 1:12-cv-22282; 11th Cir. 12-15738)

The U.S. Court of Appeals for the Eleventh Circuit determined on April 1, 2014, by a vote of two to one, that Florida's efforts to systematically purge voter registrations for noncitizens less than ninety days before the 2012 primary election was a violation of the NVRA.[291]

---

284. Project Vote v. Blackwell, 455 F. Supp. 2d 694 (N.D. Ohio 2006).

285. Mont. Democratic Party v. Eaton, 581 F. Supp. 2d 1077 (D. Mont. 2008).

286. United States Student Ass'n Found. v. Land, 585 F. Supp. 2d 925 (E.D. Mich.), *stay denied*, United States Student Ass'n Found. v. Land, 546 F.3d 373 (6th Cir. 2008).

287. Common Cause of Colo. v. Coffman, 750 F. Supp. 2d 1259 (D. Colo. 2010).

288. NVRA § 8(a)(4), 42 U.S.C. § 1973gg-6(a)(4); United States v. Missouri, 535 F.3d 844 (8th Cir. 2008); Bell v. Marinko, 367 F.3d 588 (6th Cir. 2004).

289. Arcia v. Fla. Sec'y of State, 746 F.3d 1273 (11th Cir. 2014); *see* NVRA § 8(c)(2)(A), 42 U.S.C. § 1973gg-6(c)(2)(A) (2012).

290. Project Vote/Voting for Am., Inc. v. Long, 682 F.3d 331 (4th Cir. 2012); *see* NVRA § 8(i)(1), 42 U.S.C. § 1973gg-6(i)(1).

291. Arcia v. Fla. Sec'y of State, 746 F.3d 1273 (11th Cir. 2014); *see* NVRA § 8(c)(2)(A), 42 U.S.C. § 1973gg-6(c)(2)(A).

On May 10, 2012, the *Miami Herald* reported that a study found nearly 2,700 noncitizens in Florida who were registered to vote.[292] The method of identifying noncitizens included matching voter registrations to driver's license data.[293] The suspicion that some registered voters were not citizens arose from driver's license records for persons who became citizens after they obtained their licenses to drive.[294]

In June 2012, federal complaints challenged the purge in each of Florida's three districts.

A June 8 action in the Middle District by two voters and Mi Familia Vota Education Fund challenged the purge's lack of preclearance pursuant to section 5 of the Voting Rights Act.[295] This action was dismissed on July 24, 2013, following the Supreme Court's declaring unconstitutional the section 4 criteria for the section 5 preclearance requirement.[296]

Following a June 12, 2012, complaint in the Northern District by the Justice Department,[297] U.S. District Judge Robert L. Hinkle ruled on June 27 that the NVRA's section 8(c)(2) ninety-day quiet period more sensibly applies to purges based on voters' changes in eligibility rather than registrations that were invalid from the start.[298]

---

292. Marc Caputo & Steve Bousquet, *State Finds Nearly 2,700 Noncitizens on Voting Rolls*, Miami Herald, May 10, 2012, at 1A.

293. *Arcia*, 746 F.3d at 1277; United States v. Florida, 870 F. Supp. 2d 1346, 1347–48 (N.D. Fla. 2012).

294. *United States v. Florida*, 870 F. Supp. 2d at 1347–48.

295. Complaint, Mi Familia Vota Educ. Fund v. Detzner, No. 8:12-cv-1294 (M.D. Fla. June 8, 2012), D.E. 1; Mi Familia Vota Educ. Fund v. Detzner, 891 F. Supp. 2d 1326, 1329 (M.D. Fla. 2012); *see* 42 U.S.C. § 1973c (2012) (requiring preclearance of changes to voting procedures in jurisdictions with a certified history of discrimination); Amended Complaint, *Mi Familia Vota Educ. Fund*, No. 8:12-cv-1294 (M.D. Fla. July 27, 2012), D.E. 20.

"Five Florida counties—Hillsborough, Monroe, Collier, Hendry, and Hardee—are covered jurisdictions under Section 5 of the Voting Rights Act." *Mi Familia Vota Educ. Fund*, 891 F. Supp. 2d at 1331.

296. Order, *Mi Familia Vota Educ. Fund*, No. 8:12-cv-1294 (M.D. Fla. July 24, 2013), D.E. 60; *see* Shelby Cnty. v. Holder, 570 U.S. ___, 133 S. Ct. 2612 (2013).

297. Complaint, United States v. Florida, No. 4:12-cv-285 (N.D. Fla. June 12, 2012), D.E. 2; *United States v. Florida*, 870 F. Supp. 2d at 1349.

298. *United States v. Florida*, 870 F. Supp. 2d at 1350.

Presiding over a June 19, 2012, action in the Southern District by two voters and five organizations,[299] U.S. District Judge William J. Zloch also concluded that the 90-day proscription on registration purges does not apply to purges of noncitizens.[300]

The court of appeals reversed Judge Zloch's decision:

> First, the purpose of Secretary Detzner's program was clearly to remove the names of "ineligible voters" from the Florida voter rolls. . . .
>
> Second, . . . Secretary Detzner's program was a "systematic" program under any meaning of the word. . . .
>
> . . .
>
> . . . At most times during the election cycle, the benefits of systematic programs outweigh the costs because eligible voters who are incorrectly removed have enough time to rectify any errors. In the final days before an election, however, the calculus changes. Eligible voters removed days or weeks before Election Day will likely not be able to correct the State's errors in time to vote. . . .
>
> . . .
>
> In closing, we emphasize that our interpretation of the 90 Day Provision does not in any way handcuff a state from using its resources to ensure that non-citizens are not listed in the voter rolls. The 90 Day Provision by its terms only applies to programs which "systematically" remove the names of ineligible voters. As a result, the 90 Day Provision would not bar a state from investigating potential non-citizens and removing them on the basis of individualized information, even within the 90-day window.[301]

Regulation of Volunteer Registrars

Voting for America, Inc. v. Andrade (Gregg Costa, S.D. Tex. 3:12-cv-44; 5th Cir. 12-40914; U.S. 12A266)

Over a dissent, the U.S. Court of Appeals for the Fifth Circuit held on October 3, 2013, that two provisions of Texas's voter registration laws were not preempted by the NVRA:[302] (1) The NVRA's requirement that

---

299. Complaint, Arcia v. Detzner, No. 1:12-cv-22282 (S.D. Fla. June 19, 2012), D.E. 1; *see* Amended Complaint, *id.* (Sept. 12, 2012), D.E. 57.

300. Arcia v. Detzner, 908 F. Supp. 2d 1276 (S.D. Fla. 2012).

301. Arcia v. Fla. Sec'y of State, 746 F.3d 1273, 1281–82, 1284, 1286 (11th Cir. 2014).

302. Voting for Am., Inc. v. Steen, 732 F.3d 382, 399–400 (5th Cir. 2013), *rev'g* 888 F. Supp. 2d 816 (S.D. Tex. 2012) (preliminary injunction); *see* Voting for Am., Inc. v.

registration records be available for photocopying does not preempt Texas's forbidding private deputy registrars from photocopying completed registration applications before they submit them to registrars. (2) A Texas requirement that deputy registrars hand-deliver completed registration applications does not conflict with the NVRA's requirement that states permit registration by mail, because Texas law requires county registrars to accept mailed applications even if they are sent by scofflaw deputy registrars.

In 2011, Texas amended its election laws to enhance the regulation of "volunteer deputy registrars" (VDRs).[303] VDRs are persons authorized by voter registrars to accept voter registration applications, and they are the only persons other than voters themselves, or voters' close family members, who may submit completed applications to registrars.[304] "[T]he registrar shall appoint as deputy registrars persons who volunteer to serve."[305] VDRs must complete registration training.[306]

An organization and two voters filed a federal complaint in the Southern District of Texas's Galveston Division on February 13, 2012, claiming that some of the new VDR regulations violate the U.S. Constitution and the NVRA.[307] An amended complaint on March 15 added an affiliated organization as an additional plaintiff.[308] Judge Gregg Costa issued a preliminary injunction against some of Texas's VDR regulations on August 2.[309]

Andrade, 488 F. App'x 890, 901–03 (5th Cir. 2012) (staying the preliminary injunction pending appeal).

The Supreme Court declined to vacate the stay, over Justice Sotomayor's partial dissent; the record does not reflect on what grounds she would have vacated the stay. Voting for Am., Inc. v. Andrade, 567 U.S. ___, 133 S. Ct. 99 (2012).

303. *Voting for Am., Inc.*, 488 F. App'x at 892; *Voting for Am., Inc.*, 888 F. Supp. 2d at 820, 824.

304. *Voting for Am., Inc.*, 888 F. Supp. 2d at 822–24; Tex. Elec. Code §§ 13.031–.047 (2013).

305. Tex. Elec. Code § 13.031(a).

306. *Id.* § 13.031(e); *Voting for Am., Inc.*, 488 F. App'x at 892; *Voting for Am., Inc.*, 888 F. Supp. 2d at 820, 822, 824.

307. Complaint, Voting for Am., Inc. v. Andrade, No. 3:12-cv-44 (S.D. Tex. Feb. 13, 2012), D.E. 1.

308. Amended Complaint, *id.* (Mar. 15, 2012), D.E. 8.

309. *Voting for Am., Inc.*, 888 F. Supp. 2d 816.

It is the standard record-keeping practice of the organizational plaintiffs for persons assisting them in voter registration drives to photocopy completed applications before submitting them to registrars.[310] Texas's secretary of state ruled that Texas election law prohibits such photocopying.[311] No Texas court had ruled on the matter.[312] Judge Costa, and later a motions panel for the court of appeals, agreed with a Fourth Circuit holding that section 8(i) of the NVRA requires states to make voter registration applications available for photocopying.[313] Judge Costa determined that if the public could copy the records after the registrars received them, then the deputy registrars could copy them before submitting them to the registrars.[314] The court of appeals ruled that the NVRA's requirement that the records be available for photocopying did not apply until the records were "officially received or maintained by the State."[315]

"A volunteer deputy registrar shall deliver in person, or by personal delivery through another designated volunteer deputy, to the registrar each completed voter registration application submitted to the deputy . . . ."[316] Judge Costa ruled that the NVRA requires Texas to accept registration applications from VDRs by mail.[317] Section 6(a)(1) of the NVRA requires states to accept and use mail voter registration applications.[318] The court of appeals observed that according to Texas's election code, "county registrars must accept *every* application received by mail, even those sent by VDRs in violation of the Personal Delivery Provision."[319]

---

310. *Id.* at 821.
311. *Voting for Am., Inc.*, 488 F. App'x at 902; *Voting for Am., Inc.*, 888 F. Supp. 2d at 835.
312. *Voting for Am., Inc.*, 888 F. Supp. 2d 823.
313. *Voting for Am., Inc.*, 488 F. App'x at 902–03; *Voting for Am., Inc.*, 888 F. Supp. 2d at 835–37; NVRA § 8(i), 42 U.S.C. § 1973gg-6(i) (2012); Project Vote/Voting for Am., Inc. v. Long, 682 F.3d 331 (4th Cir. 2012).
314. *Voting for Am., Inc.*, 888 F. Supp. 2d at 837.
315. Voting for Am., Inc. v. Steen, 732 F.3d 382, 399 (5th Cir. 2013).
316. Tex. Elec. Code § 13.042(a) (2013); *Voting for Am., Inc.*, 888 F. Supp. 2d at 837–38.
317. *Voting for Am., Inc.*, 888 F. Supp. 2d at 838–39.
318. NVRA § 6(a)(1), 42 U.S.C. § 1973gg-4(a)(1).
319. *Voting for Am., Inc.*, 732 F.3d at 400; *see* Tex. Elec. Code §§ 13.071–.072.

Public Availability of Voter Registration Applications
Project Vote/Voting for America, Inc. v. Long (Rebecca Beach Smith, E.D. Va. 2:10-cv-75; 4th Cir. 11-1809)

The U.S. Court of Appeals for the Fourth Circuit held on June 15, 2012, that section 8 of the NVRA's requirement of public access to "all records concerning the implementation of programs and activities conducted for the purpose of ensuring the accuracy and currency of official lists of eligible voters" extends to voter registration applications.[320]

An organization advocating voter registration filed a federal complaint in the Eastern District of Virginia's Norfolk courthouse on February 16, 2010, to vindicate its right "to inspect and copy the completed voter registration applications and related records of prospective registrants who were denied registration in the city of Norfolk, Virginia in advance of the 2008 Presidential election."[321] The plaintiff "suspected that properly completed voter registration applications submitted by qualified and eligible citizens and residents of Norfolk, Virginia, may have been incorrectly rejected by the Norfolk General Registrar."[322]

On October 29, 2010, Judge Rebecca Beach Smith ruled that the plaintiff was entitled to the registration applications.[323] She ruled that Social Security numbers, however, had to be redacted,[324] redactions that the plaintiff had sought anyway.[325] She rejected the defendants' argument that the plaintiff lacked standing to represent voting rights because the relief that the plaintiff sought from the court was public information guaranteed by section 8.[326] The court of appeals affirmed these rulings.[327]

---

320. Project Vote/Voting for Am., Inc. v. Long, 682 F.3d 331 (4th Cir. 2012); *see* NVRA § 8(i)(1), 42 U.S.C. § 1973gg-6(i)(1).

321. Complaint at 2, Project Vote/Voting for Am., Inc. v. Long, No. 2:10-cv-75 (E.D. Va. Feb. 16, 2010), D.E. 1; *see Project Vote*, 682 F.3d at 334; Project Vote/Voting for Am., Inc. v. Long, 813 F. Supp. 2d 738, 740 (E.D. Va. 2011); Project Vote/Voting for Am., Inc. v. Long, 752 F. Supp. 2d 697, 698, 700 (E.D. Va. 2010).

322. Complaint, *supra* note 321, at 2; *see Project Vote*, 752 F. Supp. 2d at 699.

323. *Project Vote*, 752 F. Supp. 2d at 704–12 (denying dismissal); *accord Project Vote*, 813 F. Supp. 2d 738 (summary judgment); *see* Project Vote/Voting for Am., Inc., 889 F. Supp. 2d 778 (E.D. Va. 2012) (denying reconsideration).

324. *Project Vote*, 752 F. Supp. 2d at 711–12.

325. Transcript at 27, *Project Vote*, No. 2:10-cv-75 (E.D. Va. July 30, 2010, filed Nov. 8, 2010), D.E. 33.

326. *Project Vote*, 752 F. Supp. 2d at 701–04.

On August 22, 2012, Judge Smith awarded the plaintiff $184,880.25 in attorney fees and costs.[327] On January 30, 2013, Judge Smith approved a consent decree implementing her rulings.[329]

Thinning Voter Registration Lists
United States v. Missouri (Nanette K. Laughrey, W.D. Mo. 2:05-cv-4391; 8th Cir. 07-2322)

The U.S. Court of Appeals for the Eighth Circuit held on July 29, 2008, that compliance by local election officials with the NVRA is relevant in determining whether the state has met its section 8 obligation to "conduct a general program that makes a reasonable effort to remove" voter registrations of ineligible voters.[330]

The Justice Department filed a federal complaint against the State of Missouri and its secretary of state in the Western District of Missouri on November 22, 2005, to "enforce the voter registration list maintenance requirements of Section 8."[331] The complaint alleged that Missouri's 116 election jurisdictions—114 counties and the cities of St. Louis and Kansas City—were not adequately thinning voter registration lists of persons who had moved or died.[332] On May 23, 2006, Judge Nanette K. Laughrey granted partial summary judgment to Missouri: "Because neither Missouri State law nor the NVRA gives the Secretary of State enforcement authority, summary judgment is granted in favor of the Defendants on those claims that seek to hold her or the State responsible for the enforcement of the NVRA against local election authorities."[333]

After the presentation of additional evidence, Judge Laughrey granted a final judgment in favor of the defendants on April 13, 2007.[334]

> To the extent the United States is attempting to impute the conduct of the [local election authorities (LEAs)] to the State of Missouri,

---

327. Project Vote/Voting for Am., Inc. v. Long, 682 F.3d 331 (4th Cir. 2012).
328. Project Vote/Voting for Am., Inc., 887 F. Supp. 2d 704 (E.D. Va. 2012).
329. Consent Decree, *Project Vote*, No. 2:10-cv-75 (E.D. Va. Jan. 30, 2013), D.E. 114.
330. United States v. Missouri, 535 F.3d 844, 851 (8th Cir. 2008); *see* NVRA § 8(a)(4), 42 U.S.C. § 1973gg-6(a)(4) (2012).
331. Complaint, United States v. Missouri, No. 2:05-cv-4391 (W.D. Mo. Nov. 22, 2005), D.E. 1.
332. *Id.* at 4.
333. Opinion, *id.* (May 23, 2006), D.E. 35, *available at* 2006 WL 1446356.
334. Opinion, *id.* (Apr. 13, 2007), D.E. 103, *available at* 2007 WL 1115204.

they have failed to explain how Missouri law or the NVRA permits the Defendant State of Missouri to be held directly responsible for the conduct of the LEAs. Under Missouri law, no statewide official can sue the LEAs to make them comply with the NVRA, so it would make no sense to conclude that the LEAs' conduct should be imputed to the Secretary of State or the State of Missouri.[335]

The court of appeals, however, held, "Although Missouri cannot be required to *enforce* the NVRA against the LEAs, any lack of LEA compliance remains relevant to determining whether or not Missouri is reasonably conducting a general program."[336]

In 2009, on remand, the Justice Department voluntarily dismissed its complaint, filed more than three years previously, because the evidence in the record "may have limited applicability to current conditions in Missouri."[337]

Canceling Voter Registrations for Seasonal Residents
Bell v. Marinko (James G. Carr, N.D. Ohio 3:02-cv-7204; 6th Cir. 02-4370)

The U.S. Court of Appeals for the Sixth Circuit concluded on March 12, 2004, that the NVRA does not prevent states from canceling voter registrations of persons ineligible to vote.[338]

The litigation resulted from efforts to thin the voting rolls of Kelley's Island, Ohio, by removing seasonal residents.[339] A voter whose wife was registered at a different address filed a federal complaint in the Northern District of Ohio's Toledo courthouse on April 19, 2002;[340] four additional plaintiffs joined an amended complaint filed on May 15;[341] another two plaintiffs joined a second amended complaint filed on July 16.[342] The plaintiffs argued that none of the events permitted by the NVRA for can-

---

335. *Id.* at 25.
336. United States v. Missouri, 535 F.3d 844, 851 (8th Cir. 2008) (quotation marks omitted).
337. Voluntarily Dismissal, *United States v. Missouri*, No. 2:05-cv-4391 (W.D. Mo. Mar. 4, 2009), D.E. 139; *see* Dismissal Order, *id.* (Mar. 9, 2009), D.E. 140.
338. Bell v. Marinko, 367 F.3d 588 (6th Cir. 2004).
339. *Id.* at 589; Bell v. Marinko, 235 F. Supp. 2d 772, 773 (N.D. Ohio 2002).
340. Complaint, Bell v. Marinko, No. 3:02-cv-7204 (N.D. Ohio Apr. 19, 2002), D.E. 1.
341. First Amended Complaint, *id.* (May 15, 2002), D.E. 16.
342. Second Amended Complaint, *id.* (July 16, 2002), D.E. 28.

celation of voter registrations had occurred for the plaintiffs.[343] Judge James G. Carr granted the first plaintiff a temporary restraining order against a presumption that the married couple could not be registered at different addresses,[344] but as to the more general claims Judge Carr ultimately granted summary judgment to the defendants.[345] On March 12, 2004, the court of appeals affirmed.[346]

Section 8 of the NVRA provides that

each State shall—

...

(3) provide that the name of a registrant may not be removed from the official list of eligible voters except—

(A) at the request of the registrant;

(B) as provided by State law, by reason of criminal conviction or mental incapacity; or

(C) as provided under paragraph (4);

(4) conduct a general program that makes a reasonable effort to remove the names of ineligible voters from the official lists of eligible voters by reason of—

(A) the death of the registrant; or

(B) a change in the residence of the registrant . . . .[347]

The court of appeals concluded,

In creating a list of justifications for removal, Congress did not intend to bar the removal of names from the official list of persons who were ineligible and improperly registered to vote in the first place. The National Voter Registration Act protects only "eligible" voters from unauthorized removal. Eligible voters, at a minimum, are those who qualify as bona fide residents of the precinct in which they are registered or wish to register to vote.[348]

The court based its conclusion on the NVRA's expressions of protections for *eligible* voters:[349] (1) a specified purpose of the NVRA is "to establish procedures that will increase the number of *eligible* citizens who register

---

343. Bell v. Marinko, 367 F.3d at 591; *Bell*, 235 F. Supp. 2d at 774–76.

344. Temporary Restraining Order, *Bell*, No. 3:02-cv-7204 (N.D. Ohio Apr. 25, 2002), D.E. 9.

345. *Bell*, 235 F. Supp. 2d 772.

346. *Bell*, 367 F.3d 588.

347. NVRA § 8(a), 42 U.S.C. § 1973gg-6(a) (2012).

348. *Bell*, 367 F.3d at 591–92 (citations omitted).

349. *Id.* at 592.

to vote,"³⁵⁰ (2) another specified purpose is "to make it possible for Federal, State, and local governments to implement [the NVRA] in a manner that enhances the participation of *eligible* citizens as voters,"³⁵¹ (3) a state is required to "ensure that any *eligible* applicant is registered to vote in an election,"³⁵² and (4) the NVRA sets limits on the removal "from the official list of *eligible* voters"³⁵³

Undeliverable Notices of New Registrations
Common Cause of Colorado v. Coffman (John L. Kane, D. Colo. 1:08-cv-2321)

U.S. District Judge John L. Kane, District of Colorado, determined on November 3, 2010, that Colorado's annulling new voter registrations when voter registration notices are returned as undeliverable did not violate section 8(d) of the NVRA.³⁵⁴

Three organizations filed a federal complaint in the District of Colorado on October 25, 2008, alleging improper purging of voter registrations in advance of the November 4 general election.³⁵⁵ After Judge Kane heard evidence and arguments on October 29, the parties negotiated a stipulated preliminary injunction.³⁵⁶ According to the stipulation, voters whose new registrations were canceled because of undeliverable notices could cast provisional ballots.³⁵⁷ In June 2009, Judge Kane ruled that Colorado had improperly refused to count three provisional ballots.³⁵⁸

Judge Kane determined that the organizations, "whose core functions include the registration of new voters and the protection of voter rights," had standing to pursue the action.³⁵⁹ However, section 8's restrictions on canceling voter registrations for undeliverable mail do not apply to the

---

350. NVRA § 2(b)(1), 42 U.S.C. § 1973gg(b)(1) (emphasis added).
351. *Id.* § 2(b)(2), 42 U.S.C. § 1973gg(b)(2) (emphasis added).
352. *Id.* § 8(a)(1), 42 U.S.C. § 1973gg-6(a)(1) (emphasis added).
353. *Id.* § 8(a)(3), 42 U.S.C. § 1973gg-6(a)(3) (emphasis added).
354. Common Cause of Colo. v. Coffman, 750 F. Supp. 2d 1259 (D. Colo. 2010).
355. Complaint, Common Cause of Colo. v. Coffman, No. 1:08-cv-2321 (D. Colo. Oct. 25, 2008), D.E. 1; *see* Amended Complaint, *id.* (Apr. 16, 2009), D.E. 46.
356. Stipulated Injunction, *id.* (Oct. 29, 2008), D.E. 14; Minutes, *id.* (Oct. 29, 2008), D.E. 15.
357. Stipulated Injunction, *supra* note 356.
358. Order, *Common Cause of Colo.*, No. 1:08-cv-2321 (D. Colo. June 26, 2009), D.E. 84, *available at* 2009 WL 1847353; *Common Cause of Colo.*, 750 F. Supp. 2d at 1267.
359. *Common Cause of Colo.*, 750 F. Supp. 2d at 1268.

initial registration process.[360] "Plaintiffs' reading interferes with Colorado's ability to confirm a registration applicant's initial residential eligibility...."[361]

The parties stipulated to dismissal of an appeal.[362]

Improperly Canceling Voter Registrations for Changes of Address
United States Student Ass'n Foundation v. Land (Stephen J. Murphy III, E.D. Mich. 2:08-cv-14019; 6th Cir. 08-2352)

The Eastern District of Michigan's U.S. District Judge Stephen J. Murphy III issued a preliminary injunction on October 13, 2008, curtailing Michigan's practice of canceling voter registrations if voter registration cards came back from the post office as undeliverable or Michigan received notice that the voter had registered to drive in another state.[363]

Three organizations filed the complaint on September 17.[364] The court of appeals denied a motion to stay the injunction on October 29.[365] The case settled on May 25, 2010.[366]

Judge Murphy determined that Michigan's rejecting voter registrations when voter registration identification cards came back undeliverable violated section 8(d) of the NVRA because the rejections did not comport with the Act's notice and waiting period requirements.[367]

(1) A State shall not remove the name of a registrant from the official list of eligible voters in elections for Federal Office on the ground that the registrant has changed residence unless the registrant—

---

360. *Id.* at 1263–64, 1272–79.

361. *Id.* at 1263–64.

362. Stipulation, Common Cause of Colo. v. Buescher, No. 10-1546 (10th Cir. Jan. 24, 2011).

363. United States Student Ass'n Found. v. Land, 585 F. Supp. 2d 925 (E.D. Mich. 2008); United States Student Ass'n Found. v. Land, 546 F.3d 373, 376, 379–80 (6th Cir. 2008) (denying stay).

364. Complaint, United States Student Ass'n Found. v. Land, No. 2:08-cv-14019 (E.D. Mich. Sept. 17, 2008), D.E. 1; *United States Student Ass'n Found.*, 546 F.3d at 378; *United States Student Ass'n Found.*, 585 F. Supp. 2d at 929; *see* Amended Complaint, *United States Student Ass'n Found.*, No. 2:08-cv-14019 (E.D. Mich. Oct. 7, 2008), D.E. 25.

365. *United States Student Ass'n Found.*, 546 F.3d at 389.

366. Dismissal, *United States Student Ass'n Found.*, No. 2:08-cv-14019 (E.D. Mich. May 26, 2010), D.E. 96; Transcript, *id.* (May 25, 2010, filed June 10, 2010), D.E. 98; *see* Settlement Agreement, *id.* (June 24, 2010), D.E. 100.

367. *United States Student Ass'n Found.*, 585 F. Supp. 2d at 937–39.

(A) confirms in writing that the registrant has changed residence to a place outside the registrar's jurisdiction in which the registrant is registered; or

 (B) (i) has failed to respond to a notice described in paragraph (2); and

  (ii) has not voted or appeared to vote (and, if necessary, correct the registrar's record of the registrant's address) in an election during the period beginning on the date of the notice and ending on the day after the date of the second general election for Federal office that occurs after the date of the notice.[368]

In addition, Michigan's practice of canceling registrations upon learning that the voter became registered to drive in another state failed to comply with section 8(d) and failed to accommodate persons who might be residents of one state for voting purposes and residents of another state for driving purposes.[369]

In settlement, Michigan agreed to amend its practices:

 4. Defendants covenant and agree not to reject or cancel an individual's voter registration solely on the ground that the individual's original disposition notice or voter identification card is returned by the Postal Service as undeliverable.

 5. Defendants further covenant and agree not to cancel an individual's voter registration on the ground that the individual surrendered his or her Michigan driver's license or state identification card and obtained a driver's license or state identification card in another state—without specific written confirmation that the individual has changed his residence for voting purposes.[370]

The parties also agreed that the defendants would pay the plaintiffs $150,000 in attorney fees and costs.[371]

---

368. NVRA § 8(d), 42 U.S.C. § 1973gg-6(d) (2012); *see United States Student Ass'n Found.*, 546 F.3d at 376–77 (quoting statute).

369. *United States Student Ass'n Found.*, 585 F. Supp. 2d at 939–41.

370. Settlement Agreement, *supra* note 366, at 3.

371. *Id.* at 5; Transcript at 6, *United States Student Ass'n Found.*, No. 2:08-cv-14019 (E.D. Mich. May 25, 2010, filed June 10, 2010), D.E. 98.

Improperly Using Changes of Address to Purge Voter Registrations

Montana Democratic Party v. Eaton (Donald W. Molloy, D. Mont. 9:08-cv-141)

U.S. District Judge Donald W. Molloy, District of Montana, opined that one party's use of change-of-address notices in counties populated by voters of the other party to challenge over 6,000 voter registrations shortly before the 2008 general election was improper political chicanery.[372] Judge Molloy denied the plaintiffs a temporary restraining order, however, because the offending party was not a state actor governed by the federal statute and the state's decision not to effectuate the scheme mitigated the immediacy of the alleged injury.[373]

The complaint was filed one month before the general election, on the last day for voter registration.[374]

Montana law specifies that upon submission of a voter registration challenge, "the election administrator shall question the challenger and the challenged elector and may question other persons to determine whether the challenge is sufficient or insufficient to cancel the elector's registration."[375] The complaint alleged that county officials were in the process of sending notices to challenged voters.[376] "Apparently in response to the filing of Plaintiffs' complaint, the Secretary of State has astutely directed the involved counties to refrain from sending the letters of challenge."[377]

The NVRA allows for a program of registration cancelation in which "change-of-address information supplied by the Postal Service through its licensees is used to identify registrants whose addresses may have

---

372. Mont. Democratic Party v. Eaton, 581 F. Supp. 2d 1077, 1081 (D. Mont. 2008).
373. *Id.* at 1080–81 ("If the State of Montana, instead of the Montana Republican Party, engaged in the conduct that has created this controversy, its actions would violate the Federal Voter Registration Act.").
374. Complaint, Mont. Democratic Party v. Eaton, No. 9:08-cv-141 (D. Mont. Oct. 6, 2008), D.E. 2; *Mont. Democratic Party*, 581 F. Supp. 2d at 1078.
375. Mont. Code § 13-13-301(3)(a) (Westlaw 2012).
376. Complaint, *supra* note 374, at 6–7.
377. *Mont. Democratic Party*, 581 F. Supp. 2d at 1080.

changed,"[378] but a state may not systematically cancel voter registrations fewer than ninety days before a federal election.[379]

Also, the Act protects "the citizen's right to vote for at least two federal election cycles while the citizen updates his or her registration information. The idea is to promote voting while allowing states, in limited circumstances and after the passage of time, to purge voter lists of lazy, incompetent or deceased voters."[380]

> A State shall not remove the name of a registrant from the official list of eligible voters in elections for Federal office on the ground that the registrant has changed residence unless the registrant ... has not voted or appeared to vote (and, if necessary, correct the registrar's record of the registrant's address) in an election during the period beginning on the date of the notice and ending on the day after the date of the second general election for Federal office that occurs after the date of the notice.[381]

Judge Molloy set a merits hearing on the plaintiffs' pleas for declaratory and injunctive relief for the action's ninth day,[382] but four days before the hearing the plaintiffs voluntarily dismissed their action on assurances that Montana would not act on the Republican Party's challenges.[383]

Improper Regulation of Voter Registration Drives
Project Vote v. Blackwell (Kathleen M. O'Malley, N.D. Ohio 1:06-cv-1628)

U.S. District Judge Kathleen M. O'Malley, Northern District of Ohio, determined on September 8, 2006, that new Ohio regulations imposed on those who conduct voter registration drives violated the NVRA's requirement that "[a]ny State program or activity to protect the integrity of the electoral process by ensuring the maintenance of an accurate and current voter registration roll for elections for Federal office shall be uniform

---

378. NVRA § 8(c)(1)(A), 42 U.S.C. § 1973gg-6(c)(1)(A) (2012); *Mont. Democratic Party*, 581 F. Supp. 2d at 1081.
379. NVRA § 8(c)(2)(A), 42 U.S.C. § 1973gg-6(c)(2)(A); *Mont. Democratic Party*, 581 F. Supp. 2d at 1081.
380. *Mont. Democratic Party*, 581 F. Supp. 2d at 1081.
381. NVRA § 8(d)(1)(B)(ii), 42 U.S.C. § 1973gg-6(d)(1)(B)(ii).
382. *Mont. Democratic Party*, 581 F. Supp. 2d at 1085.
383. Notice, Mont. Democratic Party v. Eaton, No. 9:08-cv-141 (D. Mont. Oct. 10, 2008), D.E. 15.

[and] nondiscriminatory."[384] Judge O'Malley found that additional requirements imposed for voter registration workers who were compensated—registration, training, and attestation—while not imposing the requirements on volunteers were not uniform and nondiscriminatory.[385] Judge O'Malley also found these requirements and others constitutionally deficient for chilling voter registration.[386]

The complaint was filed on July 6, 2006, and Judge O'Malley heard the injunction motion on September 1.[387] Judge O'Malley granted the injunction at the hearing and issued a written opinion one week later.[388] On February 11, 2008, after additional briefing, Judge O'Malley converted her preliminary injunction to summary judgment.[389] On March 31, 2009, Judge O'Malley awarded the plaintiffs $321,485.28 in attorney fees and costs.[390]

Section 11: Notice

The NVRA's section 11 authorizes enforcement suits by the Attorney General without a notice requirement.[391] The notice requirement for private plaintiffs depends on closeness to the next federal election: (1) within 30 days, no notice is required;[392] (2) from 30 days to 120 days out, the aggrieved person must "provide written notice of the violation to the chief election official of the State involved" 20 days before filing suit;[393] and (3) more than 120 days before a federal election, 90 days' notice is required.[394]

---

384. Project Vote v. Blackwell, 455 F. Supp. 2d 694, 703–04 (N.D. Ohio 2006); see NVRA § 8(b)(1), 42 U.S.C. § 1973gg-6(b)(1).
385. *Project Vote*, 455 F. Supp. 2d at 703.
386. *Id.* at 702–07.
387. *Id.* at 697; Complaint, Project Vote v. Blackwell, No. 1:06-cv-1628 (N.D. Ohio July 6, 2006), D.E. 1.
388. *Project Vote*, 455 F. Supp. 2d at 697–98.
389. Opinion, *Project Vote*, No. 1:06-cv-1628 (N.D. Ohio Feb. 11, 2008), D.E. 59, *available at* 2008 WL 397585.
390. Opinion, *id.* (Mar. 31, 2009), D.E. 69, *available at* 2009 WL 917737.
391. NVRA § 11(a), 42 U.S.C. § 1973gg-9(a) (2012).
392. *Id.* § 11(b)(3), 42 U.S.C. § 1973gg-9(b)(3).
393. *Id.* § 11(b)(1)–(2), 42 U.S.C. § 1973gg-9(b)(1)–(2).
394. *Id.*

The Sixth Circuit and Michigan

ACORN v. Miller (4:95-cv-45), LaPalm v. Engler (1:95-cv-184), and United States v. Michigan (1:95-cv-386) (Douglas W. Hillman, W.D. Mich.); ACORN v. Miller (6th Cir. 96-1229)

In 1997, the U.S. Court of Appeals for the Sixth Circuit held that an intervenor did not have to provide notice.[395] The Association of Community Organizations for Reform Now (ACORN) and the other plaintiffs were safe from dismissal because "Michigan had already received actual notice from ACORN [of the violation], and already made clear its refusal to comply with the Act until 'federal funds [were] made available to fully fund' the program."[396]

Section 12: Criminal Penalties

Section 12(1) specifies criminal penalties for willful voting or registration interference.[397] Section 12(2) specifies criminal penalties for fraudulent registration (subsection (2)(A)) and for fraudulent voting (subsection (2)(B)).[398] The proscribed acts overlap considerably with acts proscribed by section 11 of the Voting Rights Act.[399]

A March 24, 2014, search of electronic records in completed cases found thrity-one defendants prosecuted in eighteen cases for violating section 12. Apparently all of these prosecutions were for violation of section 12(2). One third of the defendants were prosecuted in Missouri, and one third were prosecuted in Wisconsin. Half of the rest were prosecuted in Louisiana, and the other prosecutions were in Arizona, Illinois, North Carolina, and West Virginia.

The six Louisiana defendants were prosecuted in a single 1999 case. Twenty-two of the defendants were prosecuted in the years 2003–2008, and three were prosecuted in the years 2009–2013.

---

395. ACORN v. Miller, 129 F.3d 833, 837 (6th Cir. 1997) ("the statute pertains to those who *initiate* suits"); *see* ACORN v. Miller, 912 F. Supp. 2d 976, 983 (W.D. Mich. 1995).
396. *ACORN*, 129 F.3d at 837 (second quotation alteration in original).
397. NVRA § 12(1), 42 U.S.C. § 1973gg-10(1).
398. *Id.* § 12(2), 42 U.S.C. § 1973gg-10(2).
399. 42 U.S.C. § 1973i.

The Louisiana prosecution resulted in jury verdicts of not guilty,[400] as did one of the Wisconsin cases.[401] Prosecutions against four other defendants in 2005 Wisconsin cases were voluntarily dismissed.[402] Eight prosecutions resulted in prison terms ranging from one day to two years and three months;[403] 12 prosecutions resulted in sentences of probation.[404]

One of the convictions, which was for voting while on supervised release, was affirmed in a published Seventh Circuit opinion.[405]

---

400. Docket Sheet, United States v. Edwards, No. 1:99-cr-10024 (W.D. La. Sept. 23, 1999).

401. Jury Verdict, United States v. Brooks, No. 2:05-cr-170 (E.D. Wis. Oct. 5, 2005), D.E. 16.

402. Order, United States v. Gooden, No. 2:05-cr-212 (E.D. Wis. June 30, 2006), D.E. 18; Order, United States v. Edwards, No. 2:05-cr-211 (E.D. Wis. June 13, 2006), D.E. 16; Order, United States v. Little, No. 2:05-cr-172 (E.D. Wis. Mar. 15, 2006), D.E. 23; Order, United States v. Cox, No. 2:05-cr-209 (E.D. Wis. Dec. 7, 2005), D.E. 25.

403. Judgment, United States v. Toler, No. 2:13-cr-263 (S.D.W.V. Mar. 14, 2014), D.E. 26 (two years and three months on a guilty plea); Judgments, United States v. Bland, No. 4:07-cr-763 (E.D. Mo. Mar. 14 and Aug. 22, 2008), D.E. 116 and 200 (sentences for two defendants of one year and three months and one day, respectively, on guilty pleas); Judgment, United States v. Neal, No. 4:08-cr-93 (E.D. Mo. July 25, 2008), D.E. 21 (one day on a guilty plea); Amended Judgment, United States v. Swift, No. 2:05-cr-177 (E.D. Wis. Mar. 6, 2006), D.E. 28 (three months on a guilty plea); Judgment, United States v. Passmore, No. 5:05-cr-148 (E.D.N.C. Mar. 3, 2006), D.E. 19 (six months on a guilty plea); Judgment, United States v. Prude, No. 2:05-cr-162 (E.D. Wis. Feb. 2, 2006), D.E. 38 (two years on a guilty jury verdict), *aff'd*, 489 F.3d 873 (7th Cir. 2007); Docket Sheet, United States v. Brooks, No. 3:03-cr-30201 (S.D. Ill. Oct. 24, 2003) (one year and six months on a guilty plea).

404. Judgments, United States v. Marshall, No. 4:08-cr-1526 (D. Ariz. Dec. 1, 2009), D.E. 38 and 39 (one year for two defendants); Judgment, United States v. Humphrey, No. 4:08-cr-740 (E.D. Mo. June 12, 2009), D.E. 38 (three years on an information guilty plea for mail fraud in submitting forged voter registration applications for payment of her services); Judgments, *Bland*, No. 4:07-cr-763 (E.D. Mo. June 23 to 30, 2008), D.E. 164, 180, 182, 184, 185, and 186 (two years for four defendants on guilty pleas and one year for two defendants on pleas of guilty to another count); Judgment, United States v. Anderson, No. 2:05-cr-207 (E.D. Wis. Apr. 26, 2006), D.E. 25 (one year and two months on a guilty jury verdict); Judgment, United States v. Hamilton, No. 2:05-cr-171 (E.D. Wis. Feb. 3, 2006), D.E. 12 (two years on a guilty plea); Judgment, United States v. Ocasio, No. 2:05-cr-161 (E.D. Wis. Jan. 9, 2006), D.E. 22 (one year on a guilty plea).

405. United States v. Prude, 489 F.3d 873 (7th Cir. 2007).

Conviction for Voter Fraud

United States v. Prude (Rudolph T. Randa, E.D. Wis. 2:05-cr-162; 7th Cir. 06-1425)

The U.S. Court of Appeals for the Seventh Circuit affirmed, on June 14, 2007, a conviction for violation of the NVRA by voting before the expiration of supervised release.[406]

The defendant was on supervised release for a felony forgery conviction in Wisconsin.[407] In advance of the 2004 general election, she volunteered for presidential candidates, attended rallies, and cast an absentee ballot.[408] There was evidence that she was briefed on the terms of her supervised release, but after a friend told her that she was probably not allowed to vote she made an unsuccessful attempt to withdraw her ballot.[409]

Following an investigation of voting fraud in Milwaukee, the defendant was indicted on June 28, 2005, on a single count pursuant to section 12 of the NVRA.[410] The NVRA provides for a prison term of up to five years for someone who

> (2) knowingly and willfully deprives, defrauds, or attempts to deprive or defraud the residents of a State of a fair and impartially conducted election process, by—
>
> . . . .
>
> (B) the procurement, casting, or tabulation of ballots that are known by the person to be materially false, fictitious, or fraudulent under the laws of the State in which the election is held.[411]

The defendant was convicted by a jury on September 21[412] and sentenced February 2, 2006, to two years.[413] She was released from federal prison on October 28, 2007.[414]

---

406. *Id.*
407. *Id.* at 875.
408. *Id.*
409. *Id.*
410. Indictment, United States v. Prude, No. 2:05-cr-162 (E.D. Wis. June 28, 2005), D.E. 4; *Prude*, 489 F.3d at 874; *see* NVRA § 12(2)(B), 42 U.S.C. § 1973gg-10(2)(B) (2012).
411. NVRA § 12(2)(B), 42 U.S.C. § 1973gg-10(2)(B).
412. Jury Verdict, *Prude*, No. 2:05-cr-162 (E.D. Wis. Sept. 21, 2005), D.E. 28; *Prude*, 489 F.3d at 874.
413. Judgment, *Prude*, No. 2:05-cr-162 (E.D. Wis. Feb. 2, 2006), D.E. 38; *Prude*, 489 F.3d at 874–75.
414. http://www.bop.gov (reg. no. 07884-089).

Standing

An "aggrieved person may bring a civil action in an appropriate district court for declaratory or injunctive relief with respect to [an NVRA] violation."[415]

Early in the Act's history, district courts determined that private NVRA rights of action were available to voters, but not to candidates.[416]

In 1999, the U.S. Court of Appeals for the Fifth Circuit determined that the Association of Community Organizations for Reform Now (ACORN) did not have standing to enforce the NVRA on behalf of its members, but it did have standing to enforce the NVRA on its own behalf if NVRA violations had an impact on ACORN's own efforts.[417]

Other courts have found organizational standing to enforce the NVRA on behalf of members.[418]

Many successful lawsuits to enforce NVRA obligations to provide voter registration services to persons receiving state services for persons with disabilities were brought by the National Coalition for Students with Disabilities.[419] In 2002, U.S. District Judge Norman A. Mordue, Northern District of New York, expressed doubt that the organization had real members and was not simply a way for a policy advocate to seek judicial enforcement of legislation.[420] Two days later, U.S. District Judge Richard J. Leon, District of the District of Columbia, denied the coalition stand-

---

415. NVRA § 11(b)(2), 42 U.S.C. § 1973gg-9(b)(2).

416. Scolaro v. D.C. Bd. of Elections & Ethics, 104 F. Supp. 2d 18, 29 (D.D.C. 2000); Krislov v. Rednour, 946 F. Supp. 563, 566 (N.D. Ill. 1996).

417. ACORN v. Fowler, 178 F.3d 350 (5th Cir. 1999).

418. Nat'l Coal. for Students with Disabilities Educ. & Legal Def. Fund v. Gilmore, 152 F.3d 283, *amended by* 190 F.3d 600 (4th Cir. 1998) (substituting Governor Gilmore for Governor Allen in the case name); Mont. Democratic Party v. Eaton, 581 F. Supp. 2d 1077 (D. Mont. 2008); Nat'l Coal. for Students with Disabilities v. Taft, No. 2:00-cv-1300, 2002 WL 31409443 (S.D. Ohio Aug. 2, 2002); Nat'l Coal. for Students with Disabilities Educ. & Legal Def. Fund v. Scales, 150 F. Supp. 2d 845, 849 (D. Md. 2001).

419. *Nat'l Coal. for Students with Disabilities*, 152 F.3d 283, *amended by* 190 F.3d 600; *Nat'l Coal. for Students with Disabilities*, 2002 WL 31409443; *Nat'l Coal. for Students with Disabilities*, 150 F. Supp. 2d 845.

420. Opinion at 10, 15, Nat'l Coal. for Students with Disabilities Educ. & Legal Def. Fund v. Pataki, No. 1:00-cv-1686 (N.D.N.Y. Oct. 28, 2002), D.E. 135, *available at* 2007 WL 951559.

ing to enforce the NVRA in the District of Columbia because the coalition had failed to plead an aggrieved member.[421]

In 2001, U.S. District Judge Robert L. Hinkle, Northern District of Florida, held that the coalition had "standing to assert the pertinent rights of its members."[422] At a hearing on an award of attorney fees, "facts came to light raising questions about whether anyone other than plaintiffs' attorneys had any real stake in this litigation."[423] Judge Hinkle was troubled that the coalition's attorney had brought actions on behalf of the same person in both Maryland and Florida.[424] Judge Hinkle decided not to vacate his earlier holding because there had been an intervening settlement among the parties, which Judge Hinkle regarded as a valid contract.[425]

In 2012, U.S. District Judge Robert C. Jones, District of Nevada, held that voter registration organizations did not have standing to challenge Nevada's compliance with the NVRA because they had not shown that their registration efforts had increased as a result of noncompliance.[426] An appeal is pending.[427]

The U.S. Court of Appeals for the Second Circuit did not find standing on legislature petition[428] or vote dilution[429] theories.

---

421. Nat'l Coal. for Students with Disabilities Educ. & Legal Def. Fund v. Miller, 298 F. Supp. 2d 16, 20 (D.D.C. 2002).

422. Nat'l Coal. for Students with Disabilities Educ. & Legal Def. Fund v. Bush, 170 F. Supp. 2d 1205, 1210 (N.D. Fla. 2001).

423. Attorney Fees Order at 9–10, Nat'l Coal. for Students with Disabilities Educ. & Legal Def. Fund v. Bush, No. 4:00-cv-442 (N.D. Fla. Mar. 31, 2003), D.E. 180.

424. *Id.* at 10.

425. *Id.* at 21–22.

426. Nat'l Council of La Raza v. Miller, 914 F. Supp. 2d 1201 (D. Nev. 2012).

427. Docket Sheet, Nat'l Council of La Raza v. Miller, No. 13-15077 (9th Cir. Jan. 11, 2013).

428. Amalfitano v. United States, 21 F. App'x 67 (2d Cir.), *aff'g* No. 1:00-cv-3229, 2001 WL 103437 (S.D.N.Y. Feb. 7, 2001).

429. Opinion, Kalson v. United States, No. 05-1010 (2d Cir. Dec. 27, 2005), *filed as* Mandate, Kalsson v. United States, No. 1:04-cv-6984 (S.D.N.Y. May 5, 2006), D.E. 17, *aff'g* 356 F. Supp. 2d 371 (S.D.N.Y. 2005).

Louisiana's NVRA Compliance
ACORN v. Fowler (A.J. McNamara, E.D. La. 2:97-cv-287; 5th Cir. 98-30145)

On June 10, 1999, the U.S. Court of Appeals for the Fifth Circuit determined that the Association of Community Organizations for Reform Now (ACORN) did not have standing in federal court to enforce the NVRA on behalf of ACORN's members, but it did have standing to enforce NVRA provisions neglected by the state that caused ACORN to expend extra funds in registering voters.[430]

ACORN filed its action in the Eastern District of Louisiana on January 28, 1997.[431] Judge A.J. McNamara granted summary judgment to state defendants for lack of ACORN's standing on February 3, 1998.[432] The court of appeals reversed in part.[433] The court of appeals determined that ACORN might be able to show standing based on expenditures to register voters that would otherwise already have been registered had Louisiana provided voter registration services at government offices as required by the NVRA.[434] ACORN, however, did not show its expenditures sufficiently related for standing purposes to its two other claims: Louisiana failed to include voter registration applications in its mail-in driver's license renewal forms, and Louisiana's voter registration purge procedures were improper.[435]

On remand, after additional discovery, the case settled on January 24, 2000.[436]

---

430. ACORN v. Fowler, 178 F.3d 350 (5th Cir. 1999).

431. Docket Sheet, ACORN v. Fowler, No. 2:07-cv-287 (E.D. La. Jan. 28, 1997) (D.E. 1); *ACORN*, 178 F.3d at 355.

432. ACORN v. Fowler, No. 2:07-cv-287, 1998 WL 42578 (E.D. La. Feb. 3, 1998).

433. *ACORN*, 178 F.3d 350.

434. *Id.* at 360–61.

435. *Id.* at 359–60.

436. Voluntary Dismissal, *ACORN*, No. 2:07-cv-287 (E.D. La. Jan. 24, 2000), D.E. 77; Docket Sheet, *supra* note 431.

Standing to Challenge the NVRA's Constitutionality—Vote Dilution

Edwards v. United States (Lewis A. Kaplan, S.D.N.Y. 1:04-cv-6984); Kalson v. United States (2d Cir. 05-1010)

The U.S. Court of Appeals for the Second Circuit, on December 27, 2005, affirmed a February 16 dismissal by U.S. District Judge Lewis A. Kaplan, Southern District of New York, of a constitutional challenge to the NVRA for lack of standing.[437] The plaintiff claimed that his vote would be diluted by the increase in electoral participation resulting from implementation of the Act.[438]

The plaintiff filed his original complaint on August 27, 2004, using a pseudonym.[439] On December 14, Judge Kaplan dismissed the complaint without prejudice to the plaintiff's filing an amended complaint by December 24 using his real name.[440] The plaintiff filed an amended complaint on December 23.[441]

Standing to Challenge the NVRA's Constitutionality—Communication with the State Legislature

Amalfitano v. United States (Kimba M. Wood, S.D.N.Y. 1:00-cv-3229; 2d Cir. 01-6046)

On October 16, 2001, the U.S. Court of Appeals for the Second Circuit affirmed a February 7 decision by U.S. District Judge Kimba M. Wood, Southern District of New York, that a New York citizen did not have standing to challenge the constitutionality of the NVRA.[442] The citizen's argument was that the NVRA's imposition of obligations on New York

---

437. Opinion, Kalson v. United States, No. 05-1010 (2d Cir. Dec. 27, 2005), *filed as* Mandate, Kalsson v. United States, No. 1:04-cv-6984 (S.D.N.Y. May 5, 2006), D.E. 17, *aff'g* Kalsson v. United States Fed. Election Comm'n, 356 F. Supp. 2d 371 (S.D.N.Y. 2005).

438. Amended Complaint at 2 *Kalsson*, No. 1:04-cv-6984 (S.D.N.Y. Dec. 23, 2004), D.E. 11; *Kalsson*, 356 F. Supp. 2d at 373.

439. Complaint at 2, Edwards v. United States, No. 1:04-cv-6984 (S.D.N.Y. Aug. 27, 2004), D.E. 1.

440. Order, *id.* (Dec. 15, 2004), D.E. 10.

441. Amended Complaint, *supra* note 438.

442. Amalfitano v. United States, 21 F. App'x 67 (2d Cir. 2001), *aff'g* No. 1:00-cv-3229, 2001 WL 103437 (S.D.N.Y. Feb. 7, 2001).

impaired the citizen's ability to suggest inconsistent legislation to the state's legislature.[443]

Notice Requirement for a Private Right of Action
National Council of La Raza v. Miller (Robert C. Jones, D. Nev. 3:12-cv-3169; 9th Cir. 13-15077)

U.S. District Judge Robert C. Jones, District of Nevada, held on December 19, 2012, that plaintiffs lacked standing to challenge Nevada's compliance with section 7 of the NVRA concerning provision of voter registration services to persons receiving public assistance because (1) the plaintiffs did not show that their extensive voter registration efforts had increased as a result of Nevada's alleged compliance deficits, (2) the plaintiffs did not show that any of their members were denied voter registration services as a result of the alleged compliance deficits, and (3) although the plaintiffs alleged ongoing compliance deficits, their evidence arose from a December 2011 investigation and their June 11, 2012, complaint was filed too soon after their May 10 notice of the alleged deficits to Nevada.[444]

The plaintiffs were the National Council of La Raza and two branches of the NAACP.[445] Their May 10 notice of compliance deficits gave Nevada 20 days to comply to avoid litigation.[446] Section 11(b)(2) of the NVRA grants a private right of action to an aggrieved person if a violation is not corrected "within 20 days after receipt of the notice if the violation occurred within 120 days before the date of an election for Federal office."[447] The complaint was filed on the day before Nevada's June 12 primary.[448]

Judge Jones determined that the alleged violation occurred in December 2011, more than 120 days before the election, so section 11(b)(2)

---

443. *Amalfitano*, 2001 WL 103437, at *1.
444. Nat'l Council of La Raza v. Miller, 914 F. Supp. 2d 1201 (D. Nev. 2012).
445. Complaint, Nat'l Council of La Raza v. Miller, No. 3:12-cv-316 (D. Nev. June 11, 2012), D.E. 1; *Nat'l Council of La Raza*, 914 F. Supp. 2d at 1205.
446. Complaint, *supra* note 445, at 16; *Nat'l Council of La Raza*, 914 F. Supp. 2d at 1205.
447. NVRA § 11(b)(2), 42 U.S.C. § 1973gg-9(b)(2) (2012).
448. *Nat'l Council of La Raza*, 914 F. Supp. 2d at 1211.

gave Nevada 90 days to correct the alleged deficits—September 9—before the complaint could be filed.[449]

An appeal is pending.[450]

Failure of an Organization to Allege a Member's Injury
National Coalition for Students with Disabilities Education and Legal Defense Fund v. Miller (Richard J. Leon, D.D.C. 1:02-cv-1880)

U.S. District Judge Richard J. Leon, District of the District of Columbia, determined on October 30, 2002, that the National Coalition for Students with Disabilities Education and Legal Defense Fund did not have standing to enforce the NVRA's alleged requirement that disability offices for Washington, D.C.'s Metro be designated voter registration sites, because the Fund failed to show, or even allege, that any of its members was a D.C. resident unable to register to vote because of the alleged NVRA violation.[451]

The Fund and a Maryland resident filed their complaint on September 25, 2002, against election officials in the District of Columbia and Maryland, alleging that disability services offices in those jurisdictions for the Washington Metropolitan Area Transit Authority were not providing voter registration services as required by the NVRA.[452] Judge Leon ruled that the court did not have personal jurisdiction over the Maryland official, so the court could not provide relief to the Maryland plaintiff.[453]

---

449. *Id.* at 1208–15; *see* NVRA § 11(b)(2), 42 U.S.C. § 1973gg-9(b)(2).

450. Docket Sheet, Nat'l Council of La Raza v. Miller, No. 13-15077 (9th Cir. Jan. 11, 2013) (noting that a reply brief was filed on August 8, 2013).

451. Nat'l Coal. for Students with Disabilities Educ. & Legal Def. Fund v. Miller, 298 F. Supp. 2d 16, 20 (D.D.C. 2002).

452. Complaint, Nat'l Coal. for Students with Disabilities Educ. & Legal Def. Fund v. Miller, No. 1:02-cv-1880 (D.D.C. Sept. 25, 2002), D.E. 1; *Nat'l Coal. for Students with Disabilities*, 298 F. Supp. 2d at 18.

453. *Nat'l Coal. for Students with Disabilities*, 298 F. Supp. 2d at 18–20.

Standing to Represent Disabled Students

National Coalition for Students with Disabilities Education and Legal Defense Fund v. University of Maryland at College Park (Alexander Williams, Jr., D. Md. 8:00-cv-3309)

U.S. District Judge Alexander Williams, Jr., District of Maryland, held on July 5, 2001, that an organization had standing to seek enforcement of the NVRA on behalf of its disabled student members.[454]

The National Coalition for Students with Disabilities Education and Legal Defense Fund filed a federal complaint against the university and its officials on November 6, 2000.[455] An amended complaint omitted the university as a defendant.[456]

Judge Williams granted the university summary judgment on the coalition's section 1983 claim, finding that the coalition did not have standing to represent its members' interests under section 1983.[457] Judge Williams ruled, however, that the coalition had standing to pursue its NVRA claims on behalf of its members because the stricter standing requirements for section 1983 did not apply: "Organizations are entitled to bring suit in federal district courts based upon injuries to their members and on their own behalf for injuries they have sustained."[458]

Judge Williams approved a stipulated settlement of the case on February 21, 2002.[459]

---

454. Nat'l Coal. for Students with Disabilities Educ. & Legal Def. Fund v. Scales, 150 F. Supp. 2d 845, 849 (D. Md. 2001).

455. Docket Sheet, Nat'l Coal. for Students with Disabilities Educ. & Legal Def. Fund v. Univ. of Md. at Coll. Park, No. 8:00-cv-3309 (D. Md. Nov. 6, 2000) (D.E. 1); *Nat'l Coal. for Students with Disabilities*, 150 F. Supp. 2d at 846.

456. Docket Sheet, *supra* note 275 (D.E. 11, filed Feb. 6, 2001).

457. *Nat'l Coal. for Students with Disabilities*, 150 F. Supp. 2d at 850–51; *see* 42 U.S.C. § 1983 (2012).

458. *Nat'l Coal. for Students with Disabilities*, 150 F. Supp. 2d at 849.

459. Order, *Nat'l Coal. for Students with Disabilities*, No. 8:00-cv-3309 (D. Md. Feb. 22, 2002), D.E. 100.

Florida's NVRA Compliance

National Coalition for Students with Disabilities Education and Legal Defense Fund v. Bush (Robert L. Hinkle, N.D. Fla. 4:00-cv-442)

On February 20, 2001, U.S. District Judge Robert L. Hinkle, Northern District of Florida, held that two disabled students who did not register to vote for the 2000 general election and an organization promoting the interests of persons with disabilities had standing to pursue an action against Florida election officials for failure to facilitate voter registration for persons with disabilities, as required by the NVRA.[460]

The plaintiffs filed their complaint on November 27, 2000,[461] and two days later they sought a restraining order against, among other things, certification of Florida's election results until the plaintiffs and persons like them could register and vote in the election.[462] Judge Hinkle denied the immediate relief:

> They apparently have filed their motion ex parte, without notice to any defendant.... The assertion that the court should take action affecting the 2000 presidential election (or any other election) without so much as giving notice to any adversary is plainly unfounded.
>
> ... For purposes of plaintiffs' motion for a temporary restraining order, I conclude that, if plaintiffs failed to register because of violations of the law, the time to seek any redress affecting the 2000 election was prior to that election.[463]

In declining to dismiss the action, however, Judge Hinkle concluded the following:

---

460. Nat'l Coal. for Students with Disabilities Educ. & Legal Def. Fund v. Bush, 170 F. Supp. 2d 1205 (N.D. Fla. 2001).

461. Complaint, Nat'l Coal. for Students with Disabilities Educ. & Legal Def. Fund v. Bush, No. 4:00-cv-442 (N.D. Fla. Nov. 27, 2000), D.E. 1; Nat'l Coal. for Students with Disabilities Educ. & Legal Def. Fund v. Bush, 173 F. Supp. 2d 1272, 1274 (N.D. Fla. 2001); *see* Amended Complaint, *Nat'l Coal. for Students with Disabilities*, No. 4:00-cv-442 (N.D. Fla. Dec. 1, 2000), D.E. 6.

A third student plaintiff voluntarily withdrew on December 6, 2000. Notice, *Nat'l Coal. for Students with Disabilities*, No. 4:00-cv-442 (N.D. Fla. Dec. 6, 2000), D.E. 11.

462. Temporary Restraining Order Motion, *Nat'l Coal. for Students with Disabilities*, No. 4:00-cv-442 (N.D. Fla. Nov. 29, 2000), D.E. 4; *Nat'l Coal. for Students with Disabilities*, 173 F. Supp. 2d at 1274.

463. Order at 2–3, *Nat'l Coal. for Students with Disabilities*, No. 4:00-cv-442 (N.D. Fla. Nov. 29, 2000), D.E. 5; *see Nat'l Coal. for Students with Disabilities*, 173 F. Supp. 2d at 1274.

1. "The National Voter Registration Act plainly authorizes declaratory and injunctive relief in a private enforcement action such as the case at bar."[464]
2. "[Q]ualified immunity would not shield the defendants from liability from damages for violating these clear and express provisions of the Act, assuming a private right of action for damages exists...."[465] In their motion to dismiss the action, the defendants failed to raise the issue of whether section 1983 or some other authority afforded the plaintiffs a damages action to enforce the NVRA.[466]

In May 2001, the action settled; Florida officials agreed that they would inform various Florida agencies and contractors about "obligations under Federal and Florida law pertaining to voter registration for persons with disabilities."[467]

While the parties litigated the matter of attorney fees,[468] it came to the court's attention that the plaintiffs' attorney did not know whether either individual plaintiff was a resident of Florida, entitled to vote in Florida, or registered to vote in Florida.[469] Moreover, the plaintiffs' attorney had also named one of the Florida plaintiffs in an action brought in the District of Maryland.[470] Although this called into question the court's jurisdiction to hear the action, Judge Hinkle determined that the organizational plaintiff was able to contract with the defendants for a settlement of the action.[471] Judge Hinkle awarded the plaintiffs zero attorney fees.[472]

---

464. *Nat'l Coal. for Students with Disabilities*, 170 F. Supp. 2d at 1208.
465. *Id.* at 1209.
466. *Id.* at 1208 n.1.
467. Settlement Order, *Nat'l Coal. for Students with Disabilities*, No. 4:00-cv-442 (N.D. Fla. May 30, 2001), D.E. 106; Notice of Settlement, *id.* (May 3, 2001), D.E. 97; *Nat'l Coal. for Students with Disabilities*, 173 F. Supp. 2d at 1275.
468. *See Nat'l Coal. for Students with Disabilities*, 173 F. Supp. 2d 1272 (deciding that the plaintiffs were entitled to an award of fees).
469. Attorney Fees Order at 9–11, *Nat'l Coal. for Students with Disabilities*, No. 4:00-cv-442 (N.D. Fla. Mar. 31, 2003), D.E. 180.
470. *Id.* at 10; *see* Nat'l Coal. for Students with Disabilities Educ. & Legal Def. Fund v. Scales, 150 F. Supp. 2d 845, 847–48 (D. Md. 2001).
471. Attorney Fees Order, *supra* note 469, at 20–23.
472. *Id.* at 16–18 ("Nobody was required to change any practice with respect to registration of voters. . . . Plaintiffs also have been unable to identify any . . . person who has

Candidates Lack Standing to Enforce the NVRA—District of Columbia

Scolaro v. District of Columbia Board of Elections and Ethics (Henry H. Kennedy, Jr., D.D.C. 1:96-cv-2643)

U.S. District Judge Henry H. Kennedy, Jr., District of the District of Columbia, ruled on June 14, 2000, that plaintiffs disappointed by the results of a 1996 local election did not have standing to seek injunctive relief from alleged NVRA violations that allegedly resulted in their disappointments.[473]

Two unsuccessful candidates for Georgetown's Advisory Neighborhood Commissioners in the November 5, 1996, election filed a federal complaint against the District of Columbia's board of elections on November 22 alleging that Georgetown students were improperly allowed to vote in the election.[474] The plaintiffs were defeated by Georgetown students.[475]

On November 27, U.S. District Judge Louis F. Oberdorfer ruled that the plaintiffs' claims of District law violations needed to be heard first by the District's local courts and the plaintiff's federal constitutional claims depended on how the local courts would rule.[476] Judge Oberdorfer also declined to enjoin an inquiry into allegations of voter intimidation by a successful candidate who disseminated flyers informing Georgetown students of the tax consequences of their voting in the District.[477] On September 10, 1998, the District's court of appeals ruled against the unsuccessful candidates.[478]

---

registered to vote as a result of the Settlement Agreement and judgment enforcing it."), *aff'd*, 90 F. App'x 383 (11th Cir. 2003) (table).

473. Scolaro v. D.C. Bd. of Elections & Ethics, 104 F. Supp. 2d 18, 29 (D.D.C. 2000).

474. *Id.* at 20–22; Scolaro v. D.C. Bd. of Elections & Ethics, 946 F. Supp. 80, 81 (D.D.C. 1996); Docket Sheet, Scolaro v. D.C. Bd. of Elections & Ethics, No. 1:96-cv-2643 (D.D.C. Nov. 22, 1996).

475. Scolaro v. D.C. Bd. of Elections & Ethics, 691 A.2d 77, 79 (D.C. App. 1997); *see id.* at 78 ("This case began with a student-community struggle over available parking places.").

476. *Scolaro*, 946 F. Supp. at 81–82; *Scolaro*, 104 F. Supp. 2d at 21.

477. *Scolaro*, 946 F. Supp. at 82–83; *Scolaro*, 104 F. Supp. 2d at 21.

478. Scolaro v. D.C. Bd. of Elections & Ethics, 717 A.2d 891, 897 (D.C. App. 1998) ("In sum, none of petitioners' evidence overcomes the student voters' presumptive eligibility to vote.").

After the District's local courts decided the plaintiffs' District-law claims, Judge Kennedy dismissed the plaintiffs' amended complaint.[479] With respect to the NVRA claims, "At this stage in this case's judicial odyssey, at least two years after the term of office resulting from the 1996 elections has expired, . . . [p]laintiffs lack standing to pursue those claims because the injuries they allege cannot be redressed by the relief they seek."[480]

Candidates Lack Standing to Enforce the NVRA—Illinois
Krislov v. Rednour (Elaine E. Bucklo, N.D. Ill. 1:96-cv-674)

U.S. District Judge Elaine E. Bucklo, Northern District of Illinois, ruled on September 12, 1996, that would-be candidates for federal office did not have standing to challenge Illinois's ballot access laws as in violation of the NVRA[481] because the plaintiffs were neither the U.S. Attorney General[482] nor aggrieved voters.[483]

The two plaintiffs filed ballot-access petitions to run in the March 19, 1996, Democratic primary in Illinois for the U.S. Senate and the U.S. House of Representatives.[484] A substantial number of their petition signatures were challenged, resulting in one candidate's withdrawal.[485] The plaintiffs filed a federal complaint challenging various ballot-access rules on February 5.[486] They ultimately prevailed on a claim that a residency requirement for collectors of ballot-petition signatures was unconstitutional.[487]

---

479. *Scolaro*, 104 F. Supp. 2d 18, *summarily aff'd*, Order, Scolaro v. D.C. Bd. of Elections & Ethics, No. 00-7176 (D.C. Cir. Jan. 18, 2001), *available at* 2001 WL 135857.

480. *Id.* at 29.

On August 25, 2002, Judge Kennedy awarded intervenors in defense of the District $22,636.68 in attorney fees. Order, Scolaro v. D.C. Bd. of Elections & Ethics, No. 1:96-cv-2643 (D.D.C. Aug. 26, 2002), D.E. 70, *appeal voluntarily dismissed*, Order, Scolaro v. Sinderbrand, No. 02-7116 (D.C. Cir. Dec. 24, 2002), *available at* 2002 WL 31898178.

481. Krislov v. Rednour, 946 F. Supp. 563, 566 (N.D. Ill. 1996).

482. *See* NVRA § 11(a), 42 U.S.C. § 1973gg–9(a) (2012).

483. *See id.* § 11(b), 42 U.S.C. § 1973gg–9(b).

484. *Krislov*, 946 F. Supp. at 565.

485. *Id.*

486. Docket Sheet, Krislov v. Rednour, No. 1:96-cv-674 (N.D. Ill. Feb. 5, 1996) (D.E. 1).

487. Krislov v. Rednour, 226 F.3d 851 (7th Cir. 2000).

Privacy

The privacy of driver's license records and the requirement of some public availability of voter registration records came in conflict in a case that courts resolved by holding that voter registration records collected as part of driver licensing are not motor vehicle records.[488]

Voter Registration Records Are Not Motor Vehicle Records
Lake v. White (Robert W. Gettleman, N.D. Ill. 1:07-cv-2742); Lake v. Neal (7th Cir. 08-3765)

On November 6, 2009, the U.S. Court of Appeals for the Seventh Circuit determined that because a voter registration form is not a motor vehicle record, a board of election commissioners could not be held civilly liable for releasing a motor vehicle record when it released voter registration information provided in conjunction with an application for a driver's license.[489]

The plaintiff's May 16, 2007, federal class-action complaint filed in the Northern District of Illinois alleged that the public availability of his Social Security number, name, address, and telephone number in his voter registration record violated the Drivers' Privacy Protection Act.[490] A second amended complaint filed on June 12 named a specific person as obtaining the plaintiff's "Social Security Number, name, date of birth, sex, address, former address, and telephone number" in April.[491] Judge Robert W. Gettleman dismissed the complaint on September 29, 2008, on a finding that voter registration records are not motor vehicle records.[492]

---

488. Lake v. Neal, 585 F.3d 1059 (7th Cir. 2009), *aff'g* Opinion, Lake v. White, No. 1:07-cv-2742 (N.D. Ill. Sept. 29, 2008), D.E. 60, *available at* 2008 WL 4442603.

489. *Id.*

490. Complaint, *Lake*, No. 1:07-cv-2742 (N.D. Ill. May 16, 2007), D.E. 1; *see* Violent Crime Control and Law Enforcement Act of 1994, Pub. L. No. 103-322, title XXX, 108 Stat. 1796, 2099, *as amended*, 18 U.S.C. §§ 2721–2725 (2012).

491. Second Amended Complaint, *Lake*, No. 1:07-cv-2742 (N.D. Ill. June 12, 2008); *see* First Amended Complaint, *id.* (May 29, 2007), D.E. 5.

492. Opinion, *id.* (Sept. 29, 2008), D.E. 60, *available at* 2008 WL 4442603, *aff'd*, 585 F.3d 1059.

Conclusion

In the inherently political climate of election litigation, federal courts have steered NVRA cases for more than two decades toward the statute's twin goals of expansive voter registration and voter registration integrity.[493]

---

493. *See generally* Daniel P. Tokaji, Election Law in a Nutshell 182–83 (2013).

Appendix: National Voter Registration Act (42 U.S.C. §§ 1973gg to 1973gg-10)[494]

[Section 2:] § 1973gg. Findings and Purposes

(a) Findings

The Congress finds that—

(1) the right of citizens of the United States to vote is a fundamental right;

(2) it is the duty of the Federal, State, and local governments to promote the exercise of that right; and

(3) discriminatory and unfair registration laws and procedures can have a direct and damaging effect on voter participation in elections for Federal office and disproportionately harm voter participation by various groups, including racial minorities.

(b) Purposes

The purposes of this subchapter are—

(1) to establish procedures that will increase the number of eligible citizens who register to vote in elections for Federal office;

(2) to make it possible for Federal, State, and local governments to implement this subchapter in a manner that enhances the participation of eligible citizens as voters in elections for Federal office;

(3) to protect the integrity of the electoral process; and

(4) to ensure that accurate and current voter registration rolls are maintained.

[Section 3:] § 1973gg–1. Definitions

As used in this subchapter—

(1) the term "election" has the meaning stated in section 431(1) of title 2;

(2) the term "Federal office" has the meaning stated in section 431(3) of title 2;

(3) the term "motor vehicle driver's license" includes any personal identification document issued by a State motor vehicle authority;

(4) the term "State" means a State of the United States and the District of Columbia; and

---

494. Pub. L. No. 103-31, 107 Stat. 77 (1993), *as amended.*

(5) the term "voter registration agency" means an office designated under section 1973gg–5(a)(1) of this title [NVRA section 7(a)(1)] to perform voter registration activities.

[Section 4:] § 1973gg–2. National procedures for voter registration for elections for Federal office

(a) In general

Except as provided in subsection (b) of this section, notwithstanding any other Federal or State law, in addition to any other method of voter registration provided for under State law, each State shall establish procedures to register to vote in elections for Federal office—

(1) by application made simultaneously with an application for a motor vehicle driver's license pursuant to section 1973gg–3 of this title [NVRA section 5];

(2) by mail application pursuant to section 1973gg–4 of this title [NVRA section 6]; and

(3) by application in person—

(A) at the appropriate registration site designated with respect to the residence of the applicant in accordance with State law; and

(B) at a Federal, State, or nongovernmental office designated under section 1973gg–5 of this title [NVRA section 7].

(b) Nonapplicability to certain States

This subchapter does not apply to a State described in either or both of the following paragraphs:

(1) A State in which, under law that is in effect continuously on and after August 1, 1994, there is no voter registration requirement for any voter in the State with respect to an election for Federal office.

(2) A State in which, under law that is in effect continuously on and after August 1, 1994, or that was enacted on or prior to August 1, 1994, and by its terms is to come into effect upon the enactment of this subchapter, so long as that law remains in effect, all voters in the State may register to vote at the polling place at the time of voting in a general election for Federal office.

[Section 5:] § 1973gg–3. Simultaneous application for voter registration and application for motor vehicle driver's license

(a) In general

(1) Each State motor vehicle driver's license application (including any renewal application) submitted to the appropriate State motor vehicle authority under State law shall serve as an application for voter registration with respect to elections for Federal office unless the applicant fails to sign the voter registration application.

(2) An application for voter registration submitted under paragraph (1) shall be considered as updating any previous voter registration by the applicant.

(b) Limitation on use of information

No information relating to the failure of an applicant for a State motor vehicle driver's license to sign a voter registration application may be used for any purpose other than voter registration.

(c) Forms and procedures

(1) Each State shall include a voter registration application form for elections for Federal office as part of an application for a State motor vehicle driver's license.

(2) The voter registration application portion of an application for a State motor vehicle driver's license—

(A) may not require any information that duplicates information required in the driver's license portion of the form (other than a second signature or other information necessary under subparagraph (C));

(B) may require only the minimum amount of information necessary to—

(i) prevent duplicate voter registrations; and

(ii) enable State election officials to assess the eligibility of the applicant and to administer voter registration and other parts of the election process;

(C) shall include a statement that—

(i) states each eligibility requirement (including citizenship);

(ii) contains an attestation that the applicant meets each such requirement; and

(iii) requires the signature of the applicant, under penalty of perjury;

(D) shall include, in print that is identical to that used in the attestation portion of the application—

(i) the information required in section 1973gg–6(a)(5)(A) and (B) of this title [NVRA section 8(a)(5)(A) and (B)];

(ii) a statement that, if an applicant declines to register to vote, the fact that the applicant has declined to register will remain confidential and will be used only for voter registration purposes; and

(iii) a statement that if an applicant does register to vote, the office at which the applicant submits a voter registration application will remain confidential and will be used only for voter registration purposes; and

(E) shall be made available (as submitted by the applicant, or in machine readable or other format) to the appropriate State election official as provided by State law.

(d) Change of address

Any change of address form submitted in accordance with State law for purposes of a State motor vehicle driver's license shall serve as notification of change of address for voter registration with respect to elections for Federal office for the registrant involved unless the registrant states on the form that the change of address is not for voter registration purposes.

(e) Transmittal deadline

(1) Subject to paragraph (2), a completed voter registration portion of an application for a State motor vehicle driver's license accepted at a State motor vehicle authority shall be transmitted to the appropriate State election official not later than 10 days after the date of acceptance.

(2) If a registration application is accepted within 5 days before the last day for registration to vote in an election, the application shall be transmitted to the appropriate State election official not later than 5 days after the date of acceptance.

[Section 6:] § 1973gg–4. Mail registration

(a) Form

(1) Each State shall accept and use the mail voter registration application form prescribed by the Federal Election Commission pursuant to section 1973gg–7(a)(2) of this title [NVRA section 9(a)((2)] for the registration of voters in elections for Federal office.

(2) In addition to accepting and using the form described in paragraph (1), a State may develop and use a mail voter registration form that meets all of the criteria stated in section 1973gg–7(b) of this title [NVRA section 9(b)] for the registration of voters in elections for Federal office.

(3) A form described in paragraph (1) or (2) shall be accepted and used for notification of a registrant's change of address.

(b) Availability of forms

The chief State election official of a State shall make the forms described in subsection (a) of this section available for distribution through governmental and private entities, with particular emphasis on making them available for organized voter registration programs.

(c) First-time voters

(1) Subject to paragraph (2), a State may by law require a person to vote in person if—

(A) the person was registered to vote in a jurisdiction by mail; and

(B) the person has not previously voted in that jurisdiction.

(2) Paragraph (1) does not apply in the case of a person—

(A) who is entitled to vote by absentee ballot under the Uniformed and Overseas Citizens Absentee Voting Act [42 U.S.C. 1973ff et seq.];

(B) who is provided the right to vote otherwise than in person under section 1973ee–1(b)(2)(B)(ii) of this title [Voting Accessibility for the Elderly and Handicapped]; or

(C) who is entitled to vote otherwise than in person under any other Federal law.

(d) Undelivered notices

If a notice of the disposition of a mail voter registration application under section 1973gg–6(a)(2) of this title [NVRA section 8(a)(2)] is sent by nonforwardable mail and is returned undelivered, the registrar may proceed in accordance with section 1973gg–6(d) of this title [NVRA section 8(d)].

[Section 7:] § 1973gg–5. Voter registration agencies

(a) Designation

(1) Each State shall designate agencies for the registration of voters in elections for Federal office.

(2) Each State shall designate as voter registration agencies—
   (A) all offices in the State that provide public assistance; and
   (B) all offices in the State that provide State-funded programs primarily engaged in providing services to persons with disabilities.

(3) (A) In addition to voter registration agencies designated under paragraph (2), each State shall designate other offices within the State as voter registration agencies.

(B) Voter registration agencies designated under subparagraph (A) may include—
   (i) State or local government offices such as public libraries, public schools, offices of city and county clerks (including marriage license bureaus), fishing and hunting license bureaus, government revenue offices, unemployment compensation offices, and offices not described in paragraph (2)(B) that provide services to persons with disabilities; and
   (ii) Federal and nongovernmental offices, with the agreement of such offices.

(4) (A) At each voter registration agency, the following services shall be made available:
   (i) Distribution of mail voter registration application forms in accordance with paragraph (6).
   (ii) Assistance to applicants in completing voter registration application forms, unless the applicant refuses such assistance.
   (iii) Acceptance of completed voter registration application forms for transmittal to the appropriate State election official.

(B) If a voter registration agency designated under paragraph (2)(B) provides services to a person with a disability at the person's home, the agency shall provide the services described in subparagraph (A) at the person's home.

(5) A person who provides service described in paragraph (4) shall not—

(A) seek to influence an applicant's political preference or party registration;

(B) display any such political preference or party allegiance;

(C) make any statement to an applicant or take any action the purpose or effect of which is to discourage the applicant from registering to vote; or

(D) make any statement to an applicant or take any action the purpose or effect of which is to lead the applicant to believe that a decision to register or not to register has any bearing on the availability of services or benefits.

(6) A voter registration agency that is an office that provides service or assistance in addition to conducting voter registration shall—

(A) distribute with each application for such service or assistance, and with each recertification, renewal, or change of address form relating to such service or assistance—

(i) the mail voter registration application form described in section 1973gg–7(a)(2) of this title [NVRA section 9(a)(2)], including a statement that—

(I) specifies each eligibility requirement (including citizenship);

(II) contains an attestation that the applicant meets each such requirement; and

(III) requires the signature of the applicant, under penalty of perjury; or

(ii) the office's own form if it is equivalent to the form described in section 1973gg–7(a)(2) of this title [NVRA section 9(a)(2)],

unless the applicant, in writing, declines to register to vote;

(B) provide a form that includes—

(i) the question, "If you are not registered to vote where you live now, would you like to apply to register to vote here today?";

(ii) if the agency provides public assistance, the statement, "Applying to register or declining to register to vote will not affect the amount of assistance that you will be provided by this agency.";

(iii) boxes for the applicant to check to indicate whether the applicant would like to register or declines to register to vote (failure to check either box being deemed to constitute a declination to register for purposes of subparagraph (C)), together with the statement (in close proximity to the boxes and in prominent type), "IF YOU DO NOT CHECK EITHER BOX, YOU WILL BE CON-

SIDERED TO HAVE DECIDED NOT TO REGISTER TO VOTE AT THIS TIME.";

(iv) the statement, "If you would like help in filling out the voter registration application form, we will help you. The decision whether to seek or accept help is yours. You may fill out the application form in private."; and

(v) the statement, "If you believe that someone has interfered with your right to register or to decline to register to vote, your right to privacy in deciding whether to register or in applying to register to vote, or your right to choose your own political party or other political preference, you may file a complaint with _____.", the blank being filled by the name, address, and telephone number of the appropriate official to whom such a complaint should be addressed; and

(C) provide to each applicant who does not decline to register to vote the same degree of assistance with regard to the completion of the registration application form as is provided by the office with regard to the completion of its own forms, unless the applicant refuses such assistance.

(7) No information relating to a declination to register to vote in connection with an application made at an office described in paragraph (6) may be used for any purpose other than voter registration.

(b) Federal Government and private sector cooperation

All departments, agencies, and other entities of the executive branch of the Federal Government shall, to the greatest extent practicable, cooperate with the States in carrying out subsection (a) of this section, and all nongovernmental entities are encouraged to do so.

(c) Armed Forces recruitment offices

(1) Each State and the Secretary of Defense shall jointly develop and implement procedures for persons to apply to register to vote at recruitment offices of the Armed Forces of the United States.

(2) A recruitment office of the Armed Forces of the United States shall be considered to be a voter registration agency designated under subsection (a)(2) of this section for all purposes of this subchapter.

(d) Transmittal deadline

(1) Subject to paragraph (2), a completed registration application accepted at a voter registration agency shall be transmitted to the appropriate State election official not later than 10 days after the date of acceptance.

(2) If a registration application is accepted within 5 days before the last day for registration to vote in an election, the application shall be transmitted to the appropriate State election official not later than 5 days after the date of acceptance.

Ex. Ord. No. 12926. Implementation of National Voter Registration Act of 1993

By the authority vested in me as President by the Constitution and the laws of the United States of America, including section 301 of title 3, United States Code, and in order to ensure, as required by section 7(b) of the National Voter Registration Act of 1993 (42 U.S.C. 1973gg) [42 U.S.C. 1973gg–5(b)] ("the Act"), that departments, agencies, and other entities of the executive branch of the Federal Government cooperate with the States in carrying out the Act's requirements, it is hereby ordered as follows:

Section 1. Assistance to States. To the greatest extent practicable, departments, agencies, and other entities of the executive branch of the Federal Government that provide, in whole or in part, funding, grants, or assistance for, or with respect to the administration of, any program of public assistance or services to persons with disabilities within the meaning of section 7(a) of the Act shall: (a) provide, to State agencies administering any such program, guidance for the implementation of the requirements of section 7 of the Act, including guidance for use and distribution of voter registration forms in connection with applications for service;

(b) assist each such State agency administering any such program with the costs of implementation of the Act [42 U.S.C. 1973gg et seq.], consistent with legal authority and the availability of funds, and promptly indicate to each State agency the extent to which such assistance will be made available; and

(c) designate an office or staff to be available to provide technical assistance to such State agencies.

Sec. 2. Armed Forces Recruitment Offices. The Secretary of Defense is directed to work with the appropriate State elections authorities in each State to develop procedures for persons to apply to register to vote at Armed Forces recruitment offices as required by section 7(c) of the Act.

Sec. 3. Acceptance of Designation. To the greatest extent practicable, departments, agencies, or other entities of the executive branch of the Federal Government, if requested to be designated as a voter registration agency pursuant to section 7(a)(3)(B)(ii) of the Act, shall: (a) agree to such a designation if agreement is consistent with the department's, agency's, or entity's legal authority and availability of funds; and

(b) ensure that all of its offices that are located in a particular State will have available to the public at least one of the national voter registration forms that are required under the Act to be available in that State.

William J. Clinton.

[Section 8:] § 1973gg–6. Requirements with respect to administration of voter registration

(a) In general

In the administration of voter registration for elections for Federal office, each State shall—

(1) ensure that any eligible applicant is registered to vote in an election—

(A) in the case of registration with a motor vehicle application under section 1973gg–3 of this title [NVRA section 5], if the valid voter registration form of the applicant is submitted to the appropriate State motor vehicle authority not later than the lesser of 30 days, or the period provided by State law, before the date of the election;

(B) in the case of registration by mail under section 1973gg–4 of this title [NVRA section 6], if the valid voter registration form of the applicant is postmarked not later than the lesser of 30 days, or the period provided by State law, before the date of the election;

(C) in the case of registration at a voter registration agency, if the valid voter registration form of the applicant is accepted at the voter registration agency not later than the lesser of 30 days, or the period provided by State law, before the date of the election; and

(D) in any other case, if the valid voter registration form of the applicant is received by the appropriate State election official not later than the lesser of 30 days, or the period provided by State law, before the date of the election;

(2) require the appropriate State election official to send notice to each applicant of the disposition of the application;

(3) provide that the name of a registrant may not be removed from the official list of eligible voters except—

(A) at the request of the registrant;

(B) as provided by State law, by reason of criminal conviction or mental incapacity; or

(C) as provided under paragraph (4);

(4) conduct a general program that makes a reasonable effort to remove the names of ineligible voters from the official lists of eligible voters by reason of—

(A) the death of the registrant; or

(B) a change in the residence of the registrant, in accordance with subsections (b), (c), and (d) of this section;

(5) inform applicants under sections 1973gg–3, 1973gg–4, and 1973gg–5 of this title [NVRA sections 5, 6, and 7] of—

(A) voter eligibility requirements; and

(B) penalties provided by law for submission of a false voter registration application; and

(6) ensure that the identity of the voter registration agency through which any particular voter is registered is not disclosed to the public.

(b) Confirmation of voter registration

Any State program or activity to protect the integrity of the electoral process by ensuring the maintenance of an accurate and current voter registration roll for elections for Federal office—

(1) shall be uniform, nondiscriminatory, and in compliance with the Voting Rights Act of 1965 (42 U.S.C. 1973 et seq.); and

(2) shall not result in the removal of the name of any person from the official list of voters registered to vote in an election for Federal office by reason of the person's failure to vote, except that nothing in this paragraph may be construed to prohibit a State from using the procedures described in subsections (c) and (d) of this section to remove an individual from the official list of eligible voters if the individual—

(A) has not either notified the applicable registrar (in person or in writing) or responded during the period described in subparagraph (B) to the notice sent by the applicable registrar; and then

(B) has not voted or appeared to vote in 2 or more consecutive general elections for Federal office.

(c) Voter removal programs

(1) A State may meet the requirement of subsection (a)(4) of this section by establishing a program under which—

(A) change-of-address information supplied by the Postal Service through its licensees is used to identify registrants whose addresses may have changed; and

(B) if it appears from information provided by the Postal Service that—

(i) a registrant has moved to a different residence address in the same registrar's jurisdiction in which the registrant is currently registered, the registrar changes the registration records to show the new address and sends the registrant a notice of the change by forwardable mail and a postage prepaid pre-addressed return form by which the registrant may verify or correct the address information; or

(ii) the registrant has moved to a different residence address not in the same registrar's jurisdiction, the registrar uses the notice procedure described in subsection (d)(2) of this section to confirm the change of address.

(2) (A) A State shall complete, not later than 90 days prior to the date of a primary or general election for Federal office, any program the purpose of which is to systematically remove the names of ineligible voters from the official lists of eligible voters.

(B) Subparagraph (A) shall not be construed to preclude—

(i) the removal of names from official lists of voters on a basis described in paragraph (3)(A) or (B) or (4)(A) of subsection (a) of this section; or

(ii) correction of registration records pursuant to this subchapter.

(d) Removal of names from voting rolls

(1) A State shall not remove the name of a registrant from the official list of eligible voters in elections for Federal office on the ground that the registrant has changed residence unless the registrant—

(A) confirms in writing that the registrant has changed residence to a place outside the registrar's jurisdiction in which the registrant is registered; or

(B) (i) has failed to respond to a notice described in paragraph (2); and

(ii) has not voted or appeared to vote (and, if necessary, correct the registrar's record of the registrant's address) in an election during the period beginning on the date of the notice and ending on the day after the date of the second general election for Federal office that occurs after the date of the notice.

(2) A notice is described in this paragraph if it is a postage prepaid and pre-addressed return card, sent by forwardable mail, on which the registrant may state his or her current address, together with a notice to the following effect:

(A) If the registrant did not change his or her residence, or changed residence but remained in the registrar's jurisdiction, the registrant should return the card not later than the time provided for mail registration under subsection (a)(1)(B) of this section. If the card is not returned, affirmation or confirmation of the registrant's address may be required before the registrant is permitted to vote in a Federal election during the period beginning on the date of the notice and ending on the day after the date of the second general election for Federal office that occurs after the date of the notice, and if the registrant does not vote in an election during that period the registrant's name will be removed from the list of eligible voters.

(B) If the registrant has changed residence to a place outside the registrar's jurisdiction in which the registrant is registered, information concerning how the registrant can continue to be eligible to vote.

(3) A voting registrar shall correct an official list of eligible voters in elections for Federal office in accordance with change of residence information obtained in conformance with this subsection.

(e) Procedure for voting following failure to return card

(1) A registrant who has moved from an address in the area covered by a polling place to an address in the same area shall, notwithstanding failure to notify the registrar of the change of address prior to the date of an election, be permitted to vote at that polling place upon oral or written affirma-

tion by the registrant of the change of address before an election official at that polling place.

(2) (A) A registrant who has moved from an address in the area covered by one polling place to an address in an area covered by a second polling place within the same registrar's jurisdiction and the same congressional district and who has failed to notify the registrar of the change of address prior to the date of an election, at the option of the registrant—

(i) shall be permitted to correct the voting records and vote at the registrant's former polling place, upon oral or written affirmation by the registrant of the new address before an election official at that polling place; or

(ii) (I) shall be permitted to correct the voting records and vote at a central location within the same registrar's jurisdiction designated by the registrar where a list of eligible voters is maintained, upon written affirmation by the registrant of the new address on a standard form provided by the registrar at the central location; or

(II) shall be permitted to correct the voting records for purposes of voting in future elections at the appropriate polling place for the current address and, if permitted by State law, shall be permitted to vote in the present election, upon confirmation by the registrant of the new address by such means as are required by law.

(B) If State law permits the registrant to vote in the current election upon oral or written affirmation by the registrant of the new address at a polling place described in subparagraph (A)(i) or (A)(ii)(II), voting at the other locations described in subparagraph (A) need not be provided as options.

(3) If the registration records indicate that a registrant has moved from an address in the area covered by a polling place, the registrant shall, upon oral or written affirmation by the registrant before an election official at that polling place that the registrant continues to reside at the address previously made known to the registrar, be permitted to vote at that polling place.

(f) Change of voting address within a jurisdiction

In the case of a change of address, for voting purposes, of a registrant to another address within the same registrar's jurisdiction, the registrar shall correct the voting registration list accordingly, and the registrant's name may not be removed from the official list of eligible voters by reason of such a change of address except as provided in subsection (d) of this section.

(g) Conviction in Federal court

(1) On the conviction of a person of a felony in a district court of the United States, the United States attorney shall give written notice of the

conviction to the chief State election official designated under section 1973gg–8 of this title [NVRA section 10] of the State of the person's residence.

(2) A notice given pursuant to paragraph (1) shall include—
(A) the name of the offender;
(B) the offender's age and residence address;
(C) the date of entry of the judgment;
(D) a description of the offenses of which the offender was convicted; and
(E) the sentence imposed by the court.

(3) On request of the chief State election official of a State or other State official with responsibility for determining the effect that a conviction may have on an offender's qualification to vote, the United States attorney shall provide such additional information as the United States attorney may have concerning the offender and the offense of which the offender was convicted.

(4) If a conviction of which notice was given pursuant to paragraph (1) is overturned, the United States attorney shall give the official to whom the notice was given written notice of the vacation of the judgment.

(5) The chief State election official shall notify the voter registration officials of the local jurisdiction in which an offender resides of the information received under this subsection.

(h) Omitted

(i) Public disclosure of voter registration activities

(1) Each State shall maintain for at least 2 years and shall make available for public inspection and, where available, photocopying at a reasonable cost, all records concerning the implementation of programs and activities conducted for the purpose of ensuring the accuracy and currency of official lists of eligible voters, except to the extent that such records relate to a declination to register to vote or to the identity of a voter registration agency through which any particular voter is registered.

(2) The records maintained pursuant to paragraph (1) shall include lists of the names and addresses of all persons to whom notices described in subsection (d)(2) of this section are sent, and information concerning whether or not each such person has responded to the notice as of the date that inspection of the records is made.

(j) "Registrar's jurisdiction" defined

For the purposes of this section, the term "registrar's jurisdiction" means—
(1) an incorporated city, town, borough, or other form of municipality;
(2) if voter registration is maintained by a county, parish, or other unit of government that governs a larger geographic area than a municipality, the geographic area governed by that unit of government; or

(3) if voter registration is maintained on a consolidated basis for more than one municipality or other unit of government by an office that performs all of the functions of a voting registrar, the geographic area of the consolidated municipalities or other geographic units.

[Section 9:] § 1973gg–7. Federal coordination and regulations

(a) In general

The Election Assistance Commission—

(1) in consultation with the chief election officers of the States, shall prescribe such regulations as are necessary to carry out paragraphs (2) and (3);

(2) in consultation with the chief election officers of the States, shall develop a mail voter registration application form for elections for Federal office;

(3) not later than June 30 of each odd-numbered year, shall submit to the Congress a report assessing the impact of this subchapter on the administration of elections for Federal office during the preceding 2-year period and including recommendations for improvements in Federal and State procedures, forms, and other matters affected by this subchapter; and

(4) shall provide information to the States with respect to the responsibilities of the States under this subchapter.

(b) Contents of mail voter registration form

The mail voter registration form developed under subsection (a)(2) of this section—

(1) may require only such identifying information (including the signature of the applicant) and other information (including data relating to previous registration by the applicant), as is necessary to enable the appropriate State election official to assess the eligibility of the applicant and to administer voter registration and other parts of the election process;

(2) shall include a statement that—

(A) specifies each eligibility requirement (including citizenship);

(B) contains an attestation that the applicant meets each such requirement; and

(C) requires the signature of the applicant, under penalty of perjury;

(3) may not include any requirement for notarization or other formal authentication; and

(4) shall include, in print that is identical to that used in the attestation portion of the application—

(i) the information required in section 1973gg–6(a)(5)(A) and (B) of this title [NVRA section 8(a)(5)(A) and (B)];

(ii) a statement that, if an applicant declines to register to vote, the fact that the applicant has declined to register will remain confidential and will be used only for voter registration purposes; and

(iii) a statement that if an applicant does register to vote, the office at which the applicant submits a voter registration application will remain confidential and will be used only for voter registration purposes.

[Section 10:] § 1973gg–8. Designation of chief State election official

Each State shall designate a State officer or employee as the chief State election official to be responsible for coordination of State responsibilities under this subchapter.

[Section 11:] § 1973gg–9. Civil enforcement and private right of action

(a) Attorney General

The Attorney General may bring a civil action in an appropriate district court for such declaratory or injunctive relief as is necessary to carry out this subchapter.

(b) Private right of action

(1) A person who is aggrieved by a violation of this subchapter may provide written notice of the violation to the chief election official of the State involved.

(2) If the violation is not corrected within 90 days after receipt of a notice under paragraph (1), or within 20 days after receipt of the notice if the violation occurred within 120 days before the date of an election for Federal office, the aggrieved person may bring a civil action in an appropriate district court for declaratory or injunctive relief with respect to the violation.

(3) If the violation occurred within 30 days before the date of an election for Federal office, the aggrieved person need not provide notice to the chief election official of the State under paragraph (1) before bringing a civil action under paragraph (2).

(c) Attorney's fees

In a civil action under this section, the court may allow the prevailing party (other than the United States) reasonable attorney fees, including litigation expenses, and costs.

(d) Relation to other laws

(1) The rights and remedies established by this section are in addition to all other rights and remedies provided by law, and neither the rights and remedies established by this section nor any other provision of this subchapter shall supersede, restrict, or limit the application of the Voting Rights Act of 1965 (42 U.S.C. 1973 et seq.).

(2) Nothing in this subchapter authorizes or requires conduct that is prohibited by the Voting Rights Act of 1965 (42 U.S.C. 1973 et seq.).

[Section 12:] § 1973gg–10. Criminal penalties

A person, including an election official, who in any election for Federal office—
> (1) knowingly and willfully intimidates, threatens, or coerces, or attempts to intimidate, threaten, or coerce, any person for—
>> (A) registering to vote, or voting, or attempting to register or vote;
>>
>> (B) urging or aiding any person to register to vote, to vote, or to attempt to register or vote; or
>>
>> (C) exercising any right under this subchapter; or
>
> (2) knowingly and willfully deprives, defrauds, or attempts to deprive or defraud the residents of a State of a fair and impartially conducted election process, by—
>> (A) the procurement or submission of voter registration applications that are known by the person to be materially false, fictitious, or fraudulent under the laws of the State in which the election is held; or
>>
>> (B) the procurement, casting, or tabulation of ballots that are known by the person to be materially false, fictitious, or fraudulent under the laws of the State in which the election is held,

shall be fined in accordance with title 18 (which fines shall be paid into the general fund of the Treasury, miscellaneous receipts (pursuant to section 3302 of title 31), notwithstanding any other law), or imprisoned not more than 5 years, or both.

The Federal Judicial Center

Board
The Chief Justice of the United States, *Chair*
Judge John D. Bates, Director of the Administrative Office of the U.S. Courts
Judge Catherine Blake, U.S. District Court for the District of Maryland
Magistrate Judge Jonathan W. Feldman, U.S. District Court for the Western District of New York
Judge James F. Holderman, Jr., U.S. District Court for the Northern District of Illinois
Judge Kent A. Jordan, U.S. Court of Appeals for the Third Circuit
Judge Michael Melloy, U.S. Court of Appeals for the Eighth Circuit
Chief Judge C. Ray Mullins, U.S. Bankruptcy Court for the Northern District of Georgia
Judge Kathryn H. Vratil, U.S. District Court for the District of Kansas

Director
Judge Jeremy D. Fogel

Deputy Director
John S. Cooke

About the Federal Judicial Center
The Federal Judicial Center is the research and education agency of the federal judicial system. It was established by Congress in 1967 (28 U.S.C. §§ 620–629), on the recommendation of the Judicial Conference of the United States.

By statute, the Chief Justice of the United States chairs the Center's Board, which also includes the director of the Administrative Office of the U.S. Courts and seven judges elected by the Judicial Conference.

The organization of the Center reflects its primary statutory mandates. The Education Division plans and produces education and training for judges and court staff, including in-person programs, video programs, publications, curriculum packages for in-court training, and Web-based programs and resources. The Research Division examines and evaluates current and alternative federal court practices and policies. This research assists Judicial Conference committees, who request most Center research, in developing policy recommendations. The Center's research also contributes substantially to its educational mission. The Federal Judicial History Office helps courts and others study and preserve federal judicial history. The International Judicial Relations Office provides information to judicial and legal officials from foreign countries and assesses how to inform federal judicial personnel of developments in international law and other court systems that may affect their work. Two units of the Director's Office—the Information Technology Office and the Editorial & Information Services Office—support Center missions through technology, editorial and design assistance, and organization and dissemination of Center resources.

www.ingramcontent.com/pod-product-compliance
Lightning Source LLC
Chambersburg PA
CBHW070107210526
45170CB00013B/779